DEAR TEEN ME

First published in 2012 by Zest Books
35 Stillman Street, Suite 121, San Francisco, CA 94107
www.zestbooks.net
Created and produced by Zest Books, San Francisco, CA

Typeset in Asa and Corbel

Teen Nonfiction / Social Situations & Adolescence / Biography & Autobiography

Library of Congress Control Number: 2012905455

ISBN: 978-1-936976-21-8

CREDITS
BOOK EDITOR: Daniel Harmon
CREATIVE DIRECTOR: Hallie Warshaw
ART DIRECTOR/COVER & GRAPHIC DESIGN: Tanya Napier
MANAGING EDITOR: Pam McElroy
EDITORIAL ASSISTANT: Ann Edwards
PRODUCTION EDITOR: Keith Snyder

TEEN ADVISORS: Alex Idzal, Maria Charlene Sacramento,
Marcus Dixon, Frances Saux

Manufactured in China
SCP 10 9 8 7 6 5 4 3 2 1
4500371474

All photos courtesy of the contributing authors with the exception of Jennifer Ziegler.

DEAR TEEN ME

Edited By E. Kristin Anderson
and Miranda Kenneally

—For our grandparents
And for teen readers everywhere

Dear Readers,

It started with Hanson. Yes—that band from the 90's with the three blond brothers and the hit single "MMMBop." You can giggle all you want, but they were Emily's obsession as a teen. Other kids picked on her for loving them, but she tried not to care, and only blushed a little when her classmates asked about the portrait of Taylor Hanson that she was working on that one day in art class. Growing up in Maine, Emily missed out on the opportunity to see Hanson live. (They didn't tour up there until after she'd moved away.) But at 27, Emily saw them for the first time. All grown up, they rocked hard on the stage at Antone's. It was such a rush. On the way out the door, elated to the point of slurred speech, Emily knew she had to tell her teen self about it. So she did. In a very long post on her blog.

For her part, Miranda would talk about *Star Trek* with anybody who would listen when she was a kid. Unfortunately, none of her friends liked it. They considered *Star Trek* dorky, and this destroyed her self-esteem. It wasn't until college that Miranda found other people who also loved *Star Trek*. How much would teen Miranda have loved to know that there *were* other people out there – great people! – who actually shared her interests?

The internet didn't exist back then—or at least, not like it does now. Now, kids everywhere can find friends online who share similar interests. (This is how we found each other.) When we started putting together Dear Teen Me, we wanted it to be a place for authors to share experiences with teens, so that teens would know they are not alone and that they are cared for, and that there are adults who remember what it's like to be a teen.

We began posting letters on December 1, 2010, and almost immediately, the site blew up. Or, at least, we felt like it did—the response was beyond our wildest expectations. We received messages from so many authors who wanted to write letters to their teen selves, to give hope and advice and direction based on what they knew now. And, even more importantly, readers were joining the chorus, saying "me too!" and "thanks for sharing!" and "you make me feel less alone." We laughed, we cried, and we hugged (if only virtually) every step of the way. In 2011, we met the incredible folks at Zest who said, hey, let's make a book out of this thing. This is that book.

This book is for you. For the loners, the stoners, the freaks and the geeks, the head cheerleaders and the kids eating lunch in the library, the starting lineup, the benchwarmers, the glee club, and the marching band. This book is for everyone who has ever felt alone or misunderstood, for everyone who dreads prom and also for every teen in the homecoming court. For the wimps, the Goths, and the jocks. This book is for you.

We hope you love it.

Most Sincerely,

E. Kristin Anderson and Miranda Kenneally

E K Anderson

Miranda Kenneally

CONTENTS

DEAR TEEN ME

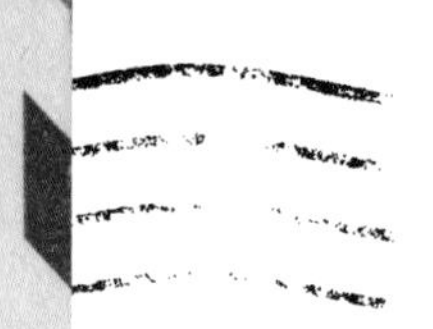

WANT. TAKE. HAVE.

E. Kristin Anderson

Dear Teen Me,

We spend most mornings writing in our diary. Not the fun diary that you share with friends. Not the one where you draw pictures of Hanson and Foo Fighters and analyze the Grammys. I'm talking about the one where you write about how scared you are that we'll never find THE ONE, and about how fighting with your mom is wearing you out, and how you're grossed out by sex, and how desperately, how *insanely* you want to date John O'Bleary*.

You barely know John O'Bleary. He transferred to your school during sophomore year, and now he's the goalie for the hockey team. The team your brother plays for. The team your dad coaches. And, yes, your dad *actually* told his players that if they tried to date you they'd be "riding the pine pony" indefinitely.

But Dad would have made an exception for John. He's different from the other hockey guys. And sometimes he and Dad talk about you on the team bus. So now you're convinced that you and John O'Bleary are going to ride off into the sunset in whatever car he drives (like I said, you barely know him) and get married and have adorable O'Bleary babies.

So just about every entry in your journal is about John O'Bleary. I mean, you're probably writing about him right now, as the sun finishes coming up. I bet there's a cup of Raspberry Zinger herbal tea cooling on your nightstand next to a half-eaten bagel slathered in cream cheese. You have a whole routine: wake up, shower, make breakfast, crawl back into bed (with your breakfast), and write in your diary. Don't even try to deny it. You're about to start another entry about how today is the day you're going to talk to John.

In fact, there are eleventy billion entries of pure O'Bleary pining. I could transcribe a page word for word, but I'd hate to betray your confidence. After all, we swore to ourselves we would never share THAT journal with anyone; we fear the damage its publication could wreak upon our impending fame. (We don't want our adoring public to know that we're so shallow we only ever write about boys.) Anyway, that's what the other journal's for:

sharing fun stuff with friends and illustrating, on a frame-by-frame basis, our delusions of grandeur.

You have a bedtime diary ritual, too. At night you crawl under the covers, pull out one of your metallic Gelly Roll pens, and woefully scribble into the same pages that you filled with hope that very morning. It goes like this:

> *I didn't talk to John today. [Insert explanation here.] I don't know what's wrong with me. I just know that there's something between us. There's a reason he transferred into school when he did. And he told Dad [insert anecdote here]. Why can't I just talk to him? I'm going to regret it if I don't. This shouldn't be so hard. But it is.*
>
> *Tomorrow I'm going to talk to John O'Bleary.*

And so it goes, time and time again...*until*: You know that dance that's coming up? The Sadie Hawkins dance, where girls are supposed to ask the boys? (As if you haven't asked your date to every other dance, you inadvertent feminist, you.) Well, you're going to go up to John and ask him to go to the dance with you. Flat out. And he's going to say that someone else just asked him—it's a girl you're kind of friends with, and one of the only popular girls who's never picked on you. So you can't even hate her. Worse still, John is so freaking nice that he asks you to save him a dance.

You never do get that dance. But here's the thing: you weren't supposed to.

I was home for Christmas in 2010, sitting on the sofa at Nini's house (yes, we still call our grandmother Nini), when she announced that John O'Bleary was marrying that very same girl who asked him to the dance not half an hour before you did. And in that moment, I couldn't help wondering what it would have been like to be Mrs. O'Bleary.

Teen Me, don't let this crush you. As I write this today, I can't help but feel lucky that I'm *not* Mrs. O'Bleary. I'm in love right now with someone else entirely, hundreds of miles from *chez* O'Bleary

But even knowing that, I still want you to ask John to that dance. You wrote in your secret journal that you didn't want to be thirty and look back with regrets. You were sure that if you didn't ask John out, you would always wonder, "What if?" I'm almost thirty now, and thanks to you, I have no what-ifs. So, asking John out? Yeah, I think we can say with certainty that it was a good idea. (Even though the journal entry from that evening says something like: *Well, stamp an* R *on my forehead and throw me in the Reject bin!*)

You're not a reject, Teen Me. You're *brave*. When you think back on that moment later on, you'll feel pride, more than anything else: pride, because you're the kind of girl who has the *cojones* to ask for what she wants.

You're setting a high standard for yourself as an adult. For *me*. You already know what you want and you ask for it without hesitation. Okay, maybe with a little hesitation—the journal proves that—but I love that you dare not only to dream, but to believe in those dreams, whatever the cost. I mean, it will be about three years before you realize that you're not going to be a rock star in this lifetime, but you're never, ever going to be afraid to (poorly) sing karaoke. And sure, you're not poet laureate (yet), but you're going to publish a lot of great poems in *actual* magazines because you will actually put those poems in the mail and send them out into the world. And no matter how many times you get your heart broken, you'll keep on believing in love.

Asking John O'Bleary to the Sadie Hawkins dance was about so much more than getting rejected by the boy of your dreams; it was about setting the pace for the rest of your life. You already believe in something Faith will say on *Buffy the Vampire Slayer*: "Want, take, have!" And while you're not going to use this for evil quite the way she did, you're going to wear your heart on your sleeve and pursue impossible goals and take inadvisable risks. Because it's the only way you know how to be you.

But I think you've already got a sense of this—even on bad days, when you feel like you have eighty R's on your forehead (like the day when you realize that, whoa, there's no cure for bipolar disorder; or all the times when you want to hide until school, and your parents, and the mean girls disappear). Pretty soon you're going to realize that "It works if you work it" is more than a Taylor Hawkins quote (from that new magazine *Nylon*). "It works if you work it" are words to live by, and you're already on top of it. So don't change a damn thing.

*Name not-so-elusively changed to protect the bashful.

E. Kristin Anderson has a fancy diploma that says "B.A. in Classics," which makes her sound smart but hasn't helped her get any jobs in ancient Rome. However, she *did* briefly work for *The New Yorker.* Currently living in Austin, Texas, Ms. Anderson is an assistant editor at *Hunger Mountain.* With Miranda Kenneally, she founded DearTeenMe.com, the blog upon which this book was based. As a poet she has been published in dozens of literary magazines all over the world. She wrote her first trunk book at sixteen. It was about the band Hanson, and may or may not still be in a notebook at her parents' house. Look out for Ms. Anderson's work in *Coin Opera II* (forthcoming), a collection of poems about video games from Sidekick Books.

CONTENTS UNDER PRESSURE

Jessica Lee Anderson

Dear Teen Me,

It's your senior year of high school, 8:00 p.m. on a Friday night. There's a huge football game happening right now and parties are just getting started. Sadly, you're in bed. Not because you have some illness or because you're nursing a hangover or anything like that (though be warned: you will soon suffer the worst hangover of your life). You're just exhausted. So very, very exhausted.

You've been averaging about five hours of sleep per night—actually less with midterms and the SAT looming. Plus, you have a ton of other projects due, like that student council environmental proposal you grudgingly signed up for because it was going to look good on your college and scholarship applications. To date, you've filled out twenty-nine applications. You're *desperate*. You want to go away to college badly, but support and finances are limited. These obstacles make you even more obsessed.

In addition, you feel shattered after finding out that your boyfriend and best friend have started seeing each other behind your back. Yes, you've been crazy busy, but this is inexcusable. The betrayal makes you feel even more exhausted. Before crawling into bed, you thought about calling someone to confide in, but who would you call? Some people at school consider you "popular," but they don't know the real you. They only know the people-pleasing Jessica—the one who wishes everyone would like her.

You just want to hibernate until graduation. And while you don't physically slow down, your spirit seems to withdraw as time progresses. Days blur together from so many simultaneous responsibilities—projects, quizzes, finals, additional applications, club meetings, volunteering opportunities, etc. Plus you have to take the ACT because you choked during the SAT. Despite your ongoing exhaustion, you manage to attend a few parties and football games, but you continue with the people-pleasing façade. You let your guard down with that cute guy from advisory, but then you try to distance yourself emotionally because dating someone now isn't part of your plan.

Amazingly, the college acceptances start rolling in, and you receive quite a few scholarships. You're elated—you've accomplished the seemingly impossible! This amazing feeling is temporary, though, and the desperation doesn't dissipate. If anything, you put more pressure on yourself as you prepare for college and your future. I wish that your adult self—me—could intervene and tell you that it's not right to make success your god. Unfortunately, it takes a breakdown before you'll be able to realize this.

You sign up for eighteen hours of classes during your first semester at college, plus join a couple of clubs and take on a part-time job. This is more than you can handle, and you're near the point of flipping out. So when you get an opportunity to party in Mexico with some new friends, you're all for a chance to escape. With each sip from a bottle of gin, you feel layers of your veneer cracking, and your anxiety lessening. Losing control feels good—until you completely lose it.

Let me just say that there's nothing like a police-escorted trip to the hospital to make you rethink your priorities. You will recover from this worst hangover of your life, and your soul will start to heal too (albeit a bit more slowly than your black eye). While there are many things you can control, you need to learn to let go in more appropriate ways. Try losing yourself on long hikes, or while writing.

And by the way, that cute guy from advisory? You'll marry him.

Jessica Lee Anderson

Jessica Lee Anderson is the author of *Trudy* (winner of the 2005 Milkweed Prize for Children's Literature), *Border Crossing* (a 2009 Quick Picks Nomination), and *Calli* (a 2011 Reader's Choice Nomination). She's published two nonfiction readers, as well as fiction and nonfiction for a variety of magazines including *Highlights for Children*. Visit JessicaLeeAnderson.com for more information.

Dear Teen Me,

IT'S SO AWESOME + HILARIOUS, TOO, LIKE AFTER THE ALIENS SEND BUCKAROO THIS SECRET FORMULA AND HE DOESN'T HAVE ANY PAPER SO HE WRITES IT ON HIS HAND AND THEN HE SHOWS IT TO THE PROFESSOR AND SAYS "WHAT'S THIS?" + THE PROFESSOR SAYS, "WHY IT'S YOUR HAND, BUCKAROO." AND THEN JOHN LITHGOW SAYS...

(((PING)))

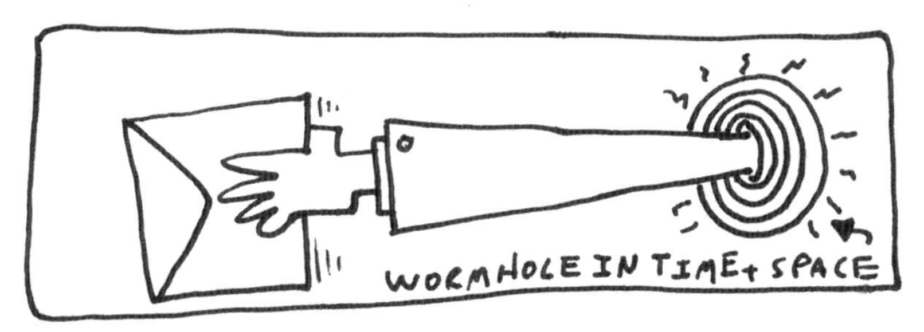

COMEDIC PAUSE...

WHAT?!? YOU'VE NEVER GOTTEN A LETTER FROM THE FUTURE??? IT'S SO AWESOME! FIRST THERE'S THIS "PING" AND THEN AN ARM COMES THROUGH A HOLE..

Tom Angleberger eventually discovered that he was supposed to write down all that nerdy stuff instead of saying it out loud, and now he's the author of *Horton Halfpott* (2011), *Fake Mustache* (2012), and the Origami Yoda series.

FRAME ME AND NAIL ME TO THE WALL

Sean Beaudoin

Dear Teen Me,

Is it possible that this arty self-portrait was ever really me? When you close your eyes, you can almost smell the incense. This shot was taken before digital cameras existed. Back then film was expensive, complicated, and difficult to process. Remember when you got into buying old cameras at the Salvation Army and then sending away to someplace in New Jersey for obsolete types of film? It's hard to tell if that was an inspired hobby or just the product of sheer, crushing boredom. In any case, this particular shot that I'm looking at now was taken with a 1950s Polaroid camera. (You paid three dollars for it and then ruined forty dollars' worth of film learning how to use it.) Apparently, there's a fine line between nerd-rock cover art and self-indulgent pretentiousness.

First, you found some "really cool lighting" in which to linger. Then you practiced getting just the right facial expression: anguished, hip, tough, and worldly (read: non-virginal). The absurdly heavy camera sat atop the tripod that you asked for (and actually got) for Christmas. There was a thumb switch at the end of a long cord that released the shutter.

Click. Flash. Genius.

You laid the exposures out on the linoleum floor like a hand of solitaire, and for some reason you decided that this one was the best. How do I know? Because now it's the only one left. How many drawers and shoe boxes and apartment closets has it sat at the bottom of? How many moves and fires and storage-space purges did it survive? In retrospect, this shot may not be the artistic breakthrough it once seemed, but there's no question it epitomizes your guiding internal mantra that year: *Things Are So Very Difficult, But I Guess I'll Deign to Persevere.*

Also, it echoes that old Depression-era truism that "nothing truly good ever happens unless it happens under light spilled through a dirty venetian blind."

Teen Me, all I can say is that I miss you dearly. I miss your white teeth. Your "go ahead and dare me to cut it off" ponytail. The red Yukon suit you wore all winter as an anti-fashion fashion statement. Not to mention the vampiric longing in your expression—an expression that seems to say, at one and the same time: "I want to create!" and "I want to be famous!" and "Do I look cool from this angle?" and "Deep down I know I'm a fraud."

You may not have had a lot of self-confidence back then, but you did at least believe—truly and honestly—that art was everywhere (at least potentially): in a sculpture made out of tires, in a poem written on a napkin, in a black-and-white photograph of a dead bird, in a song written in an hour, or in a collage of supermodel heads torn from fashion magazines and glued to the cover of your never-opened Algebra II textbook. It was a liberating and exhilarating feeling to recognize that (lowercase) art was around every corner, just waiting to be made or discovered. Back then, everything was a tool, including (and especially) yourself: cameras, clay, pens, glue, crayons, your voice, or a guitar. The idea of *potential* practically swirled through the air—a cluster of insistent notes that made up the backbeat of almost everything connected with you at seventeen.

Teen Me, I would love to be you again, even for just an hour.

Because during that hour I would write the first fifteen chapters of a dystopian novel about a debutante vampire with a shopping addiction, bet heavily on the Super Bowl, pen an app that discourages people from using the word *app* in a sentence, and marry Natalie Portman.

And still have ten minutes to spare, just hanging out, you and me.

Plenty of time to knock out two or three more masterpieces.

Sean Beaudoin

Sean Beaudoin is the author of the novels *Going Nowhere Faster* (2007), *Fade to Blue* (2009), *You Killed Wesley Payne* (2011), and the forthcoming duo *The Infects* (fall 2012) and *Wise Young Fool* (spring 2013.) He can be found at SeanBeaudoin.com, and can also be Liked and Loved on Twitter and Facebook.

REINVENTING ME

Charles Benoit

Dear Teen Me,

Just dropping in to let you know that your little plan actually works. Sure, it seems crazy, and it doesn't start off well at all, but overall you'll be pleasantly surprised about how it turns out.

I'm stunned you ever came up with something like this in the first place. You certainly have reason enough to try—I mean, *something* has to happen—but we both know that "doing things" was never your specialty. But not doing things? In that respect you're a pro. Not talking to girls, not watching what you eat, not caring how you look, not standing up for yourself, not trying in class—nobody does nothing better than you.

And that's why the plan seems so impossible. I mean, it's one thing to say you want to change your hair; it's another thing entirely to say you're going to change everything about yourself—the way you look, the way you dress, the way you talk, who you talk to, what you talk about, what you watch, what you listen to, and where you plan to go on Friday night. Everything. And you've given yourself two months to do it. That's your plan, anyway: the ultimate makeover. If it works—and given your track record, you have no reason to think it will—you'll start tenth grade as a whole new person. And if it fails, well, you're used to that.

Granted, you have friends and you have a great (sometimes strange) family, but admit it: you aren't happy. You can picture the guy you want to be. We're not talking superpowers or sudden musical genius; all you want is to be the guy who *doesn't* say something stupid every time he opens his mouth, the one who *doesn't* get picked last for everything, who *doesn't* let jocks push him around, and who *does* know what to say to girls. To put it simply, you just don't want to be you anymore.

So you make a list. The cool of James Bond, the wit of Steve Martin, the quiet toughness of Bruce Lee. Then you write up a bunch of little plays—literally write them out—planning what you'll say when you sit down at a table of hot girls, revising the lines till you know that they'll work. You do this for every possible situation, from the jocks in the back hall to the ninth-grade algebra teacher who you'll have to face again soon. What, maybe twenty scripts or so?

Then it's off to the mall for a new look, and then over to the music store to buy the albums you *really* want—mostly early punk stuff—and before you know it, school is back in session and it's showtime!...

...where you proceed to get mocked and abused even worse than before.

But somehow you stick to the plan, and before long, it starts to get better. You gain confidence; people see that you're funny (in a good way, for once). You start taking karate and you don't embarrass yourself when you have to fight. And what do you know, by the end of the first quarter, you actually have a girlfriend. Your plan is so crazy that it actually works.

And you're still at it today, constantly trying to improve yourself, to be better tomorrow than you were today. You don't write out the scripts anymore—I can't remember the last time you didn't know what to say—and sometimes you even catch a beer with the guys who used to pick on you the most. Things changed because you made them change. Pretty impressive for a dork.

See you in few decades.

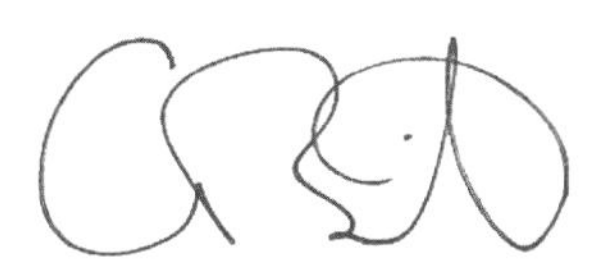

Charles Benoit is the author of *You* (2010) and *Fall from Grace* (2012), as well as several adult mysteries. When he's not hosting his radio show or busting out the ska on his tenor sax, he works as a copywriter at an ad agency. He and his wife, Rose, live in exotic Rochester, New York. Paparazzi-quality details at CharlesBenoit.com.

9 THINGS YOU NEED TO KNOW

Robin Benway

Dear Teen Me,

✶ 1. Let's just start by ripping off the Band-Aid. You need to let your bangs grow out. I'm serious. Half of your teenage life (that's a rough estimate, but I feel like it's accurate) will be spent trying to straighten them and the other half will be spent worrying that they're frizzing up, so just grow them out now. You're welcome.

✶ 2. High school stops mattering the second you graduate from it. Crazy, I know, but it's true! Remember how upset everyone was when you ~~were too lazy~~ forgot to file your paperwork for the National Honor Society? Or when your Spanish teacher got mad because you ditched her class so many times? It turns out that nobody cares whether or not you were an honors student, and your Spanish skills turn out to be quite stellar—especially when asking for directions in Spain when you're thirty-two. (Yes, you go to Spain. And Italy and France, too. Start packing now.)

✶ 3. That boy in your chemistry class isn't just being friendly. He's *flirting* with you. The sooner you can figure out the difference between the two, the easier your life will be. And you really need to talk to Chemistry Boy more, because on the last day of senior year, he will write a beautiful sentence in your yearbook that involves him using the word "perpetually" correctly—and it will be the most awesome thing that has ever happened to you. So far.

✶ 4. You pick amazing friends. All those girls you hang out with at lunchtime? You'll still be hanging out with them when you're all in your thirties. They'll still make you laugh until you have to pee, and they'll be the first ones to call you when things go horribly wrong. (Oops, spoiler alert!)

✶ 5. Right before your senior year of high school, your house will flood while you're on vacation with your family and you'll come home to a total disaster. You'll have to live with your mother and younger brother in a hotel room for the next three months, and while it seems insane at the time, the three of you will become closer than ever before as a result. They will turn out to be two of your best friends, and you'll find yourselves laughing and reminiscing about that experience time and time again. Believe it or not, it actually becomes a funny story. And while you survive the hotel experience intact, you'll never find that one sweater again.

★ 6. That being said, before you go on vacation, CHECK TO MAKE SURE A PIPE HASN'T BURST BEFORE LEAVING THE HOUSE. SERIOUSLY. GO CHECK.

★ 7. Six weeks after you turn eighteen, you'll move to New York City to attend NYU and live in Greenwich Village. Sounds awesome, right? Like a dream come true? Well, you'll cry like a baby for the entire first week, and then you'll feel so homesick that you'll construct elaborate fantasies about taking a cab to the airport and flying home. Don't. Stay for at least two years. It's good for you to be in a new city with new people. You'll learn how to ride the subway and tell the difference between the express and local trains. And after eighteen years in Orange County, California, you'll finally discover what "winter" really means. (Helpful hint: buy a sturdy umbrella, but don't bother with a hat. You look ridiculous in hats.) If you leave too soon, you'll miss walking through Washington Square Park after a January storm, seeing the bare trees filled with flecks of icy light, and feeling the contentment that comes from knowing you're exactly where you ought to be. You'll miss that exciting night at the diner when, for reasons that are never made entirely clear, your waiter has to run outside to punch a passerby while you huddle with the rest of the customers in the back of the restaurant, waiting for the police to arrive. (Now *that* is a story for another time. But don't tell Mom about it until you're a lot older. She'll freak.)

★ 8. There's going to be a period in your life where everything goes wrong. It just does. I'm sorry. Your grandparents will pass away. Your dad is going to die. You'll become very sick and have to quit your awesome PR job at the bookstore. You'll also get rejected from all your MFA programs on the same day. I can't sugarcoat it; it's just going to suck. You'll cry a lot, and when you start working again you'll think that you've screwed everything up, that everything you want to achieve will never happen. You'll be ashamed of your life.

Please, don't worry. You worry enough as it is. All these seemingly wrong turns are actually leading you in the right direction. All those things you want to achieve are just ahead of you, so don't you dare stop reaching for them. They're closer than you realize, and if you stop, if you give up and give in, then all that struggle will have been wasted.

★ 9. You're going to write the following in your journal on January 23, 1996: "The ideal life for me right now would be to live in a nice, sunny apartment in either New York or Los Angeles, with a PowerBook and my cat, and just write whenever I feel like it." (Yes, I read your journal. Hope that doesn't make things awkward between us. And you have lovely penmanship, by the way. Enjoy it while it lasts.)

Look, I don't want to give too much away, but one day, that journal entry will be important to you. (Except for the cat part. Why did you write that? You've never liked cats. Get a dog instead.) So relax. Take some deep breaths. You know how you spend every morning of senior year listening to music in the car before your first class? That's okay. It turns out that a lot of your classmates are doing the exact same thing. And that one English teacher who hints that you don't take your work seriously? You'll never hear his name again, so don't get all worked up about it. Just put that voodoo doll down.

You know how Mom is always saying, "Everything works out"? She's right. It'll take some time, but you'll get there. And the journey isn't all that bad either.

Buckle up, kid. You're going to have an amazing life...just as soon as you grow out your bangs.

Robin Benway

Robin Benway is the author of *Audrey, Wait!* (2009) and *The Extraordinary Secrets of April, May & June* (2010). She lives in Los Angeles with her beloved dog and her equally beloved espresso machine.

Q and A:

WHAT WAS YOUR MOST EMBARRASSING MOMENT?

"Failing gym class."

Jennifer Rush

~

"Letting a friend talk me into wearing those orange overalls to her house, only to discover it was my surprise birthday party. All night in those things. Ugh."

Mary Lindsey

~

"In 8th grade, I was singing a solo at church, and my knees locked and I fainted in front of everyone."

Miranda Kenneally

~

"Oh, so many. How about the time I fell down the stairs at the theatre in a dress and flashed everyone? Let's start there."

Jessica Corra

~

"My first kiss. Awful."

Ellen Hopkins

~

"There were too many to count, but maybe going up to a cute new dude named Jon and asking him if I could "draw him" for my art class. He was like, "uh... what?""

Heather Davis

~

"Washing up on a crowded beach naked. (Adventures in Skinny Dipping Gone Wrong.)"

Jess Rothenberg

~

"My whole life from ages 11-13 was one large embarrassing moment."

Lauren Oliver

~

"When my (up to that point) lifelong crush told me I had a mustache in front of all our friends. I wanted to die. Where's the facial hair bleach when you need it??"

Nikki Loftin

~

"Spending an entire day with the back of my dress tucked into my pantyhose. (And, really, "Wearing pantyhose to high school" should be the answer here, shouldn't it?)"

K.A. Holt

~

"I had a lot of them that I've clearly blocked out, but having my dress bodice tear open at dinner before junior prom wasn't my proudest moment."

E. Kristin Anderson

~

"Misspelling "seamen" in a sports article for the school paper."

Cynthia Leitich Smith

~

"Just one? I'll have to say the first time I asked a boy on a date. He said no, he couldn't, and I asked, "Why not?" My friend yelled at me later for asking that."

Tera Lynn Childs

~

"Being told that my crush only kissed me because he thought I expected him to."

Jessica Spotswood

"I should have been embarrassed by lots of stuff, but somehow, nothing trumped when my mom would introduce herself to my friends in a leopard print bikini."

Erika Stalder

"It involves a boob graze at a school dance and an ensuing letter declaring my undying love for aforementioned boob-grazer who, I learned about five minutes too late, did not reciprocate my feelings, despite our intimate connection on the dance floor."

Sarah Ockler

"Getting caught kissing at the shopping plaza by my aunt. (I was supposed to be at the library)."

Dave Roman

"Anytime I was at a party, at school, or in any social situation trying to talk to people. I always felt stupid and ugly."

Tracy White

"I had a hole in my jeans and my friend Marty ran past me, stuck his hand in the hole and literally ripped my pants off in the middle of the hall. I repeat: I was in my underpants in the middle of the hall."

Geoff Herbach

"I guess I was so embarrassed, I blocked it out."

Ilsa J. Bick

THE KNIFE

Ilsa J. Bick

Dear Teen Me,

No, you're not imagining things. What you've found squirreled under a clutch of garden tools is very real. So, go on, pick it up. Just move that hedge clipper and the hammer...and then slip it out—quiet, quiet, quiet...

God, it's *heavy*. No blood, though.

Well, of course not, you *idiot*. He'd be smart enough to clean it. God, you can be so dumb sometimes—and what now?

This is like Lois Lane always nosing around, or Lana Lang. (Does anyone know what happened to her? One day—*poof*—Clark's just suddenly an adult? Did Superboy even go to college?) You can't remember who snooped around Bruce Wayne's mansion, but you understand why someone would. Everybody loves a good mystery. It's like Zorro or the Lone Ranger: *Who's the man behind the mask?*

So *this* is like *that*. Only, instead of Clark or Bruce, that masked man—the guy with no past, the one you've wondered about for years (because, let's face it, he's *dangerous*)—well, this time, he's your dad.

But what the hell is he doing with a Nazi knife?

***

This is not the way your day was supposed to go.

As a rule, Saturdays are about helping your father. Whether or not you want it that way, that's the way it is. For your folks, chores are a kind of one-hand-washes-the-other thing. *We all work in this house. There's no such thing as a free ride.* (Like getting born was something you asked for, just to get a complimentary breakfast and a free ride somewhere.)

It's never *Ilsa, you're reading; isn't that nice.* Or *Of course, honey, go play—and here's some money for ice cream, my treat.* No. Instead, it's always: *You know, your father is out there, and* (never mind that it's five-hundred-thousand degrees) *you need to get out there and help.*

Your father routinely gives himself heat stroke, or at least comes close. In fact, that's what's happening right now: he's in the house, stretched on the sofa, a cool washcloth over his forehead, and all because you're an ungrateful wretch who *chained* this grown man to a lawn mower—because, as we all know, *he's only doing this for you.*

Let's face it. Your father is bit of a maniac. This guy…Let's just say there's a lot of drama. Dad is…well, mainly he's a bully. And you? You're *an idiot, stupid, a dummy, a moron…*and *what were you thinking, you jackass?*

He also has a tendency to explode. When he does, it means slaps, smacks, and spankings. And it happens a lot. Back then, this was acceptable behavior because every kid needed a good wallop now and then. One time, when your mom came at you with a shoe you just laughed, because she hit like a girl.

Your father is a different story.

Well, strike that: You're not sure what your dad's story is, to tell the truth. His past is a black hole. He says he doesn't remember, but you think that's crap. (In three years, you'll say *bullshit*, but right now that's a pretty dangerous word, and you're a good girl.)

I mean, seriously, get real.

Who forgets Nazis?

***

This is all they've told you: Your dad was six—or maybe seven—when the Nazis came. His house was in Alsace-Lorraine; or no, it was Schneidach; no, your half-cousin said it was in Munich. Anyway, the Nazis took them all: mom, dad, grandmother, and your father—then just a little kid. The family bounced around from camp to camp to camp.

Then…everyone died. Well, everyone except your dad. Somehow he ended up in Delaware. The rest of his family was gassed in Auschwitz. Period, end of story.

When you ask for more, you're told there is none. Dad doesn't remember… No, he doesn't want to talk about it…No, no, it was all so long ago, and anyway, don't you have some homework to do?

Some things don't add up. For one thing, your dad doesn't have a tattoo. You've looked. For another, your dad loves German shepherds and Mercedes-Benzes, and what gives with *that*?

Only...your dad also guards his food. He really does. And talk about a *temper.* A couple times, your mom's had to pull him off you. Once, you even thought he was going to hammer *her.* Step out of line and everyone pays.

So there's this dangerous guy with no past...And now, as a result, you've made up stories to fill the gaps. He and his father were resistance fighters; no, they broke out of camp; no, his father *smuggled* your dad out so that he could continue the fight on his own. It's all a little fuzzy, but you've turned your father into Batman, Superman, and the Lone Ranger.

And now, right there, is the knife that proves it.

***

Here's what you do.

You leave the knife and, flushed with excitement, run inside: *Dad, Dad, I found this knife, this Nazi knife!*

***

This is what *they* do.

Your mother freezes. Your father stares at you from the couch. Neither says a word. There's a very long moment, a very pregnant moment, when you wonder if you should repeat what you've just said. Maybe your dad didn't understand? Maybe heat stroke cooked his brain?

Then your father sits up, very slowly, and swings his legs down. "Let me check this out," he says. "You stay here."

He heads for the garage; your mom stays mum; and you do what you're told. But you're beside yourself. You've been vindicated: *Yeah, s'plain* that, *Lucy!* Finally, the family room door opens again and you look up, thrilled, because now he will *have* to tell...

But his hands are empty.

"Where is it?" You're almost tempted to look behind his back, like you did when you were little and he made things *poof* for peek-a-boo. Later, you duck out to the garage yourself, and when you don't find anything you start to wonder if maybe you really are the idiot that he says you are. "Dad, where's the knife?"

"There is no knife," he says. His face shuts down. "You made a mistake. There's nothing out there at all."

***

That is where this memory ends, like a film that's been snipped before the third reel. You never forget the knife, though, despite the fact that for the next forty years they'll continue to deny it ever existed in the first place. When they finally *do* fess up—many years later—they say: *Oh, we didn't think you needed to know about that.*

Some stories don't end as conclusively as we'd like them to, I guess. But now you're a shrink. You understand how much your dad's survival has cost him, and you understand the necessity of the fictions that both of your parents still have to tell themselves in order to keep on living.

Today, what you wish you could tell that poor twelve-year-old kid—the one who spent so many years hurting, and doubting herself, and feeling so damned stupid it took a superhuman effort some days just to breathe—is this: all the people who come after your dad now to get his story—the historians, the scholars, the merely curious—they just don't get it.

What the Nazis did to your father lives in him, and always will. That kind of damage is permanent.

But this is important. Pay attention now. What your parents did *then* was not about protecting *you*. It was about protecting *him*. And that makes you stronger than him. It makes you better. It means...the truth about that knife is yours, too. Never swallow a lie and ask for seconds. Don't believe a story that isn't yours. Your words are the knife, real and tangible, and they carry a terrible weight. You are the author of your life, and the knife is yours.

It is yours.

Ilsa J. Bick is a child psychiatrist as well as a film scholar, a surgeon wannabe, a former Air Force major, and an award-winning author of dozens of short stories and novels, including the critically acclaimed *Draw the Dark* (2011), *Ashes* (2011)—the first book in her YA apocalyptic thriller trilogy—and *Drowning Instinct* (2012). Ilsa lives with her family and other furry creatures near a Hebrew cemetery in rural Wisconsin. One thing she loves about the neighbors: they're very quiet and only come around for sugar once in a blue moon. Visit her at IlsaJBick.com.

DANCE DANCE REVOLUTION

Marke Bieschke

Dear Teen Me,

You've just turned sixteen, and pretty soon, on a random Saturday night, you're going to roll your mom's car out of the garage, start it up down the street, and sneak off to a tiny downtown Detroit nightclub. That night is going to change your life. And no, it's not because on your way back you make an illegal left-hand turn into the police chief's personal car and get totally busted for taking the car without permission—although that certainly throws a monkey wrench into your summer plans.

But that night, with two misfit friends at your side, you discover an underground world where you're accepted for the fantastic little freak that you are—a world that expresses itself though music, fashion, and dance like you've never heard or seen before. It's full of outrageous and outspoken weirdos who love art and books as much as you do, and who want to hear what you actually think about things. This world is completely opposed to your everyday high school reality, where people beat you up because you dye your hair and listen to bands from England.

You'll end up sneaking out again and again, of course. You'll spend your days fantasizing about the next club night, figuring out what you're going to wear, what you're going to say, and how you're going to dance—not to mention how you're going to get there. You've finally found a place where you belong! (And where you're not the only one who's gay.) You treasure every second in this world, and eventually it won't just be your passion; it will be your career.

Looking back, however, you realize something else: Taking the car and getting caught were part of a pattern of behavior that was more or less directly tied to your father's alcoholism. You had no clue what was going on at the time—your mother's largely successful attempts to hide his disease will implode a year later, when your dad shocks you and your sister by bravely and successfully checking into rehab. He didn't beat you or anything, and you were always provided for. But he did shut you out in weird ways—ways that made you feel you had to struggle to be heard, and that amplified both your loneliness and your independence.

You knew *something* was going on, but what? By taking the car you were crying out for attention in a perfectly teenage way, but you were also escaping an incomprehensible situation, trying to break the silence about something you felt sure was there, but which was never discussed. You were looking for a family that could openly express itself.

In a way, the whole experience was a good thing. It all turned out okay—great, even. Your father has been alcohol-free for almost twenty-five years now, and the two of you have grown close. When you were struggling with your own chemical dependency issues, his recovery served as a model for your own. When some of the dear friends you met at the club that fateful night started getting sick with AIDS, you recognized the harmful effects of silence and started speaking out. You've learned to trust your instincts, and you know that friendship and success are there for you, as long as you have the courage to reach out for them.

Marke Bieschke, aka Marke B., is a coauthor of *Queer: The Ultimate LGBT Guide for Teens* (2011). He's the managing editor of the *San Francisco Bay Guardian* and writes the weekly nightlife column Super Ego. His writing has appeared in the Best American Music Writing series, and he covers dance music for *XLR8R* magazine. He lives in San Francisco with his husband and goes out clubbing almost every night, although he no longer dyes his hair.

FIRST KISS...ISH

Joseph Bruchac

Dear Teen Me,

You didn't believe that what your grandmother kept telling you would ever come true. You couldn't. But when you hit your growth spurt you *really* hit it. Suddenly, you were bigger and stronger than all of the guys who used to bully you. You'd been fired after your first day as a caddy because you couldn't lug a golf bag, but now you're the right tackle on the football team, and a varsity heavyweight wrestler.

However, I'm sad to say that despite the growth spurt that transformed you from a bullied brainiac into a major jock, you're still not about to get the girl anytime soon. Partly, yes, because you lack smoothitude, but also because you're not willing to settle for just anybody. Your grandmother taught you to respect women as actual human beings (and not to look at them as objects), and you learned that lesson well. Your grandmother was one of the first women to pass the bar in New York, and even though she never worked as an attorney, she definitely knew how to "lay down the law" on your behavior.

In the eternal meantime, you're on your own, and you are not getting it on.

It's senior year after a big game. You're eating pizza at DeGregory's Restaurant with your football buddies. Someone comes in and says in an excited whisper: "Linda S. is in a car out back. She's drunk and willing to make out with anybody."

Linda S. is a pretty blonde girl two years younger than you, a shy country kid who lives only a mile from you. You don't remember getting up or going through the door, but the next thing you know you're in the alley beside that car. You push past two other guys, grab skinny Sammy Carson by his belt and toss him to the side. But then, instead of climbing into the back of that wide-seated '58 Buick, you take Linda S. by the arm and lead her, her on unsteady legs, to your car. Other guys step aside when they see that look in your eye.

She's crying now. You give her your handkerchief. As she leans against the car door you remember what she looked like five years ago when she was playing hopscotch, all skinny-legged and gangly, on the sidewalk outside School Two.

You drive her home. The light outside the old farmhouse reveals the fact that her mother's been waiting up for her. You walk her to her door, and she kisses your cheek and whispers, "Thank you," before she goes in. It's your first kiss—although you won't realize that or even value what it means until a lot later.

What I like about you in that memory is not just what you did, but the way you did it. You didn't think of yourself as a hero. You didn't do it to prove anything. In fact, for many years afterward you wonder what was really going on in your head back then: Did you have the urge to climb in that car with Louise yourself? (You didn't.) Did you do the right thing? (You did.)

If you had to define what you were feeling at that moment, it was probably sadness, more than anything else. Until this letter you've never mentioned what happened that night to anyone—not to the guys who avoided you as you walked down the hall on Monday morning, not to Linda S., not even to your grandmother (even though you know she'd have been proud of the way you followed the path she put you on). But you didn't do it for her approval. You did it for the person you wanted to become.

Joseph Bruchac lives in the same house in the Adirondack foothills town of Greenfield Center, New York, where he was raised by his grandparents. He's the author of more than 120 books, ranging from picture books to plays, nonfiction, poetry, and novels for middle school, high school, and adult readers. His writing often reflects his Abenaki Indian heritage. That is even true of his new YA novel *Wolf Mark* (2011), a paranormal thriller with an American Indian take on shape-shifting.

TRUST IS AS IMPORTANT AS LOVE

Jessica Burkhart

Dear Teen Me,

You're eighteen, and you don't trust anyone. Your father—an abusive con man—taught you that lesson. His fraudulent investment schemes, in which he used you and your family as bait, made you profoundly suspicious of other people's motives. But hold on: An opportunity to escape is coming. The thing is, it depends on something you don't really have—trust.

The next year, your life gets both better and worse simultaneously. You get a book deal. Your editor, Kate, becomes your best friend—she becomes the big sister you never had. The connection is immediate—one you've never had with anyone before. Soon, you love each other. You never question this. Even though Dad swore no one would ever love you, someone does.

Every day he talks about how your only responsibility is to "the family." He says that nothing is more important; nothing should make you want to leave. And frankly, it seems impossible to you that you could ever manage to get away from him.

But Kate's going to tell you something unbelievable: She wants to help you escape.

You have one opening. You say yes to Kate's offer. You're supposed to go from Florida to New York with just a single suitcase. No Mutzie (the stuffed puppy you slept with every night); no dog-eared copies of your precious Black Stallion books; no photos of your brother.

I know that this decision will seem to be the hardest part, but I'm afraid it's not. You wobble—and the fear almost destroys you. You won't be able to eat or sleep for weeks.

You try to act like nothing's up. You write around the clock, watch *General Hospital*, and play video games with your brother. Dad continues to snatch your paychecks from the mailbox before you even see the envelopes.

When you call Kate, you tell Dad it's for business. From your closet, you whisper into the phone, hoping she won't detect the doubt that's in your voice.

But of course she does. Kate knows that you want to leave with all your heart, but she also senses that you may still back out at the last second.

Days before your scheduled departure, Kate calls, and her voice—which is usually so warm and gentle—is chilly now, and the words she speaks are even colder. If you don't follow through, she says that she will still be your friend, but she won't listen to complaints about your father anymore. She won't subject herself to accounts of how a person she loves has credit cards in her name that she's not allowed to use, how she can't drive anywhere alone, and isn't allowed to speak to the neighbors—not after she gave you a chance and you didn't take it. She will love you, be your editor, and support you, but it won't be like it was before. You swear you're going to leave. Promise profusely. Kate says that she'll believe you when you get on the plane.

You cry. Hard. Hot tears. You hate her for saying those things. Support was what you needed. Or at least, that's what you thought then. Now you know that she gave you exactly what you needed. Kate terrified you in a way that no one else ever had—not even Dad. Losing her wasn't an option.

That phone call gets you on the plane. Months later, Kate tells you how she agonized over that awful call, cried when she hung up, and hated every second of speaking to you that way. But threatening your friendship was the only way to ensure your safety.

One terrible phone call saved your life. And now, you've gotten away. You are no longer kept.

Jessica Burkhart

Twenty-four year old **Jessica Burkhart** (Jess Ashley) lives in Brooklyn, New York. She is the author of the twenty-book Canterwood Crest series. Jess is also working on *Kept*, a YA verse novel based on this essay and her post on DearTeenMe.com. With her Canterwood editor and BFF, Kate Angelella, Jess co-owns Violet & Ruby—a two-person book packager. Visit Jess online at JessicaBurkhart.com.

THANK YOU, OILY PIZZA

Josh A. Cagan

Dear Teen Me,

The cafeteria pizza at BU is disgusting, but you and the kids you're hanging out with eat it because it's Friday night and hey, you're freshmen. You're wearing a plastic *Dick Tracy* movie-tie-in hat. (You're trying to make that your "thing.")

I'm sure you've noticed that I said "the kids you're hanging out with," and not "your friends." Your friends are a distant, candy-coated memory.

Why you're even hanging out with these kids is a mystery, because as far as you're concerned, nobody likes you. You're not doing great in class, and nobody else wants to talk about cartoons and Muppets—instead, they want to talk about Shakespeare and Chekhov. Everyone else came from fascinating places, they've had amazing lives, and they seem like they were born into a life in the theater.

You're some boring guy from a boring suburb.

So for the first part of your freshman year, you try to communicate to everyone at all times that YOU ARE DIFFERENT AND SPECIAL. If you could wear a gold dookie chain around your neck that said that, you would. (Although you probably would have spray-painted it black first. You wear a lot of black, hoping you can make that your "thing.")

You wear a different pair of crazy sunglasses every day of the week, hoping you can make that your "thing."

You never work with other students unless it's absolutely demanded of you, and instead you present bombastic monologues about murder and loneliness, hoping you can make that your "thing."

You work your ass off to prove to people that you are awesome, smart, edgy, and talented. You work harder at that than you do at any actual schoolwork, harder than you even work on your own art. Whether you know it or not, *this* is what has actually become your "thing."

Still, thank God you live in a dorm. Because regardless of your social status (real or imagined), if you have two dollars to throw toward pizza, you can sit in some other kids' room and eat some of that pizza. So yeah, the cafeteria pizza at BU is disgusting, but you and the kids you're hanging out with eat it, because it's Friday night and you're freshmen. And despite my earlier warning, you're still wearing that plastic "Dick Tracy" hat. (Don't get me started.)

You take a wad of napkins and begin to blot the orange grease off of your slice. Then you look at the wad of napkins and say out loud (but mostly to yourself), "I should just rub this on my face and cut out the middleman."

Everyone looks at you like the dog just talked.

And then they laugh. It's your first real laugh at college. You probably don't think much about it, but trust me, this is HUGE.

Because for the first time in your college career, you didn't open your yap to complain about how nobody understands you, or how everyone is so phony, or to brag about how many pairs of sunglasses you own.

You observed something that was funny to you, and you said it. Not because you thought it would be the coolest thing to say, not because you thought it would make people think you were brilliant, but just because you were being yourself.

And as it turned out, you being yourself made people like you. It still does.

In other words, you finally found your "thing."

Thank heavens. That hat was ridiculous.

Teen Me.

Josh A. Cagan @joshacagan co-wrote 2009's *Bandslam*, which received a 90% Fresh rating from Top Critics on RottenTomatoes.com. He also developed and co-wrote the 2001 animated series *Undergrads*. Recently, CBS Films optioned his adaptation of Kody Keplinger's *The Duff*, with McG producing. He is paid to write jokes and stories with his friends, so in other words, he lived happily ever after. He lives in Hollywood with his wife, Kayla, and their stuffed animals.

THERE'S NO SUCH THING AS IMPOSSIBLE

Riley Carney

Dear Teen Me,

You know that dream you've always had? The one about becoming an author? I'll let you in on a secret: It does happen. You make it happen.

But it's not going to be easy. You're still stuck in high school right now. I remember what it was like, and I know exactly how you feel—it seems like the whole thing is one big game; that you'll never find your place; that you'll never get away from the drama.

Like with your "best" friend. You helped her with her homework, you were nice to her, and you provided an easy boost to her self-esteem. She never really cared about you, though. Once, she even handed out Christmas presents in front of you and conveniently forgot to give you one. And I also remember what it was like on that school trip where you had to sleep in the top bunk above feuding friends who were crying hysterically. The drama is everywhere, and no matter how hard you try to avoid it, you can't seem to get away.

You're getting tired of eating lunch alone in the library just so you don't have to wander through the rows of tables at the cafeteria until you find a place to sit. You're tired of people who just want to use you for homework help. You're tired of the box that has been built up around you, tired of the walls that keep you trapped, that keep you from becoming the person who you really are inside, rather than the person who everyone thinks you are.

But in less than a year, everything will change. You'll find a way to break free of that box by doing something you've always loved. Writing will be your outlet. You're going to write a book—a book that you've been dreaming about for years. You are going to pour your heart and soul into that book, and it's going to be published. Over the next three years, you'll speak at schools all over the country, something you never thought you would have the courage to do.

But there's something you have to realize before you can break free: The box that you're in is only as strong and only as real as you believe it to be.

For so many years your peers have tried to label you, to tell you what you can and cannot do. And you believed them. You accepted what they said. You stopped believing in yourself.

You stopped believing in your dreams.

But little by little, you'll realize that the box doesn't have to exist. Once you start writing seriously, you'll discover yourself, and you'll realize that no one else has the power to dictate your own choices and your dreams.

You're the only one who can decide your future. You're the only one who can choose the person you want to be.

So, Teen Me, it's up to you. It only takes a little confidence, a little daring, and a willingness to risk failure to tear down those walls. Don't be afraid to reach for that impossible goal. Embrace it instead.

You never know where the impossible might take you.

Riley Carney

Riley Carney is, at the time of printing, eighteen years old. She is the author of the fantasy adventure series, *The Reign of the Elements.* She wrote all five books when she was fifteen and sixteen. At fourteen, Riley founded a nonprofit children's literacy organization, Breaking the Chain, because she believes that the way to break the cycle of poverty and exploitation is through education. You can learn more at RileyCarney.com and LinkByLink.org.

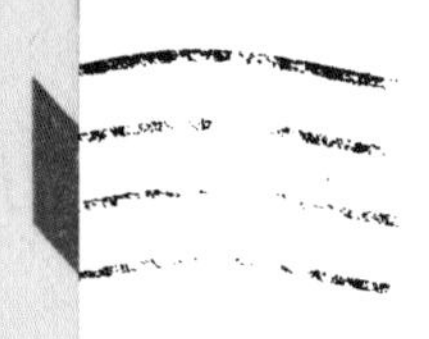

THE FUTURE ISN'T EVERYTHING

Tera Lynn Childs

Dear Teen Me,

You've always been a planner. From the time you first broke out the box of crayons to design an elaborate rabbit house—despite the fact that you didn't even have a rabbit yet—to all the hours you spent in high school plotting out your college years, designing your dream house, and even just figuring out how you could get to college early so you'd be able to meet your favorite basketball player, you've kept the future squarely in your sights.

You're always thinking ahead to the next step—and that's great—but good planning also means planning in moderation. The future isn't everything. Sometimes you sacrifice today by thinking about tomorrow. You need to slow down and spend some time in the moment, because there are a lot of things that you can't plan for, and lots of problems that planning can't solve....

Planning can't keep you young. You'll only be a teenager once, and you should enjoy the fun and freedom of those years while you can. As you get older your body will start to miss those days. So enjoy them to the fullest, and make lots of great memories.

Planning won't determine your career. You will spend countless hours planning for potential careers. Among the many career paths you'll consider are architect, lawyer, environmental biologist, marine biologist, teacher, actress, professional tennis player, theater designer, historic preservationist, veterinarian, and dozens of other ideas you won't even remember twenty years from now. In the end, you'll find your passion in something you never ever considered as a potential career plan. I won't spoil the discovery by telling you what it is, but you'll love it.

Planning can't replace people or experiences. Sometimes you get frustrated by your situation, and at other times you take the things in your life for granted. This is normal teenage angst, but on the great big scale of things, your life is pretty great. You have parents and an extended family who love you. You have great friends, a roof over your head, food on your table, and a car—embarrassing or not—to drive to school and wherever else you need to go.

It's so easy to be dissatisfied with your life, to wish for and plan for better things, but take a moment to look at the things you already have. They're pretty awesome.

So the next time you sit down to map your path out of town or to design your dream house, stop and look around. There are fun times to be had, friends and family to enjoy, and in the end your path in life will come as a complete surprise anyway. Think about the future as it comes up—when you're applying to college or picking your class schedule for the school year—and then put it aside again. Take time to enjoy the present, because it will be gone before you know it.

Tera L. Childs

Tera Lynn Childs is the award-winning author of the mythology-based *Oh. My. Gods.* (2008) and *Goddess Boot Camp* (2009), the mermaid tales *Forgive My Fins* (2010), *Fins Are Forever* (2011), and *Just for Fins* (2012), and a new trilogy about monster-hunting descendants of Medusa, starting with *Sweet Venom* (2011) and *Sweet Shadows* (2012). She has also e-published two fun chick-lit romances, *Eye Candy* and *Straight Stalk.* Tera lives nowhere in particular. She spends her time writing wherever she can find a comfy chair and a steady stream of caffeinated beverages.

THE PRINCIPAL'S OFFICE

Jessica Corra

Dear Teen Me,

She may have saved your life.

Big Bern—excuse me, Sister Bernard Agnes—isn't the chatty type. Remember when she yelled at the entire football team? Seriously, she's not to be messed with. The vice principal may be the school disciplinarian, but Big Bern is the one to fear.

She's tall and broad and imposing and *no one* wants to get called to her office. You never thought you had any reason to worry, really, but all of a sudden at the end of your sophomore year, they call your name on the loudspeaker. And you have no idea why. You tremble a little as you sit down. You've talked with this woman before, because you're a goody-two-shoes and she's asked you to help with projects from time to time, so maybe that's the reason. You don't know of anything you could have made a mess of, but maybe you've forgotten something.

She lays it out for you: She heard you wanted to transfer to the public school, and she wants to ask you why. Shifting on the hard plastic chair to avoid the full force of her attention, you have to admit that you're miserable at this tiny private school. High school was supposed to be a new leaf, but it never turned over. You've never felt like you fit in, and you sure don't have any friends. In fact, outside of your time spent at the community theater with the public school kids, you're pretty depressed. And even the theater isn't going so well right now. You're horrified to say this, and you're not even sure why you do. But you tell her the truth.

You both sit in silence for a moment, but then Big Bern simply suggests that you go to the school library. That's all she says: "Try the library." She isn't motherly, she isn't sympathetic, but she is awfully insightful. You go to the library.

The library aides are bookworms and they welcome you immediately. You find your tribe there, and you stay put. This turns out to be a good thing, since you'll be bullied out of the theater in a couple of months for dating the guy everyone else had a crush on. But by then, you'll have made lifelong friends—friends who are weird in a lot of the same ways that you are, who are into magic, and who have already discovered an essential lesson that you'll soon learn: that life is what you make of it. And that goes for school, too (whichever school it may be).

It turns out that, despite appearances, you really *were* in trouble when you got called into the principal's office. You couldn't see it, but Big Bern could.

I don't want to know what would've happened if she hadn't pointed you in the right direction, if you'd ended up alone and lost in the public school when things tanked with your theatre friends. It's not important. What *is* important is that you listened to someone and grabbed the lifeline you needed. Asking for help when you need it isn't weakness; neither is accepting help when you don't think you do. Don't be afraid to do that, again and again.

Jessica Corra

Jessica Corra is the author of *After You* (currently set to publish in the spring of 2013), a magical realism novel about sisters and sacrifices. Jessica believes in magic and chocolate cake, and is only nominally crazy. She goes on adventures in the Philadelphia area, and you can find her online at JessicaCorra.WordPress.com.

RAISING ME

Heather Davis

Dear Teen Me,

It's not easy raising yourself and your sisters, and it's not fair. Even all these years later, as I look back at all you're going through, it still makes me mad. What kind of a mother bails out on her daughters?

The day your parents told you they were getting divorced you were secretly happy that you and your sisters would be living with Dad, but you had no way of knowing that Mom was going to move out of town. And then out of state. And then out of your lives altogether.

You had no way of knowing that your grandmother would be the one to take you to be fitted for your first bra. She would have to be the one to buy you that massive box of feminine pads (which would sit on your shelf, untouched, for what seemed like forever).

You had no way of knowing that your dad would come to rely on you to take care of your younger sisters. That you would be the responsible one. The one who doesn't want to let anyone down. The one who your sisters look up to and then later resent—after all, you're more than a sister, but less than a parent.

But you don't blame Dad—how could you? He's a single parent, coming into his own true identity away from Mom, trying his best to help you along the way. If anything, you should give him a hug and tell him that you understand. Years later, he'll be one of your very best friends.

You're in the toughest part of it all right now. During these teen years, your mother will blow into town every once in a while to ask personal questions and observe you like you're some kind of science experiment: Did you get your period yet? Are you shaving your legs now? Did you pluck your eyebrows?

And even though it makes you uncomfortable, you answer, because she is your mother. You answer because you feel you should. You answer because you don't want to disappoint her—which is so messed up, because all the while she's the one who's disappointing you.

And she'll take this personal information that she extracts from you and lord it over your father. She tells him about the private things she's mined as if they prove she's still involved, that she knows something personal—something you were clearly too embarrassed to share with Dad. During these drop-ins she usually takes you to the movies. She tells you she loves you. And then she leaves. Over and over again, she leaves.

You feel powerless to say, "You have no right to me." You feel helpless to tell her to leave you the hell alone. That she is a stranger now.

Over time, her appearances confuse your understanding of what it means to love and be loved. You begin to accept that words don't have to match actions. That sometimes love is a thing bargained for with silence. You start to crave that kind of love, which is a devaluing and insidious one. This craving will stick with you for years. It's something you'll have to learn to overcome.

Keep doing your best. Right now, your little sisters need you. And, I promise you, even if it's many years from now, someday you will know real love. The kind where words match actions. The kind that doesn't leave you hanging. The kind that never lets you go.

Heather Davis

Heather Davis is the author of the novels *Never Cry Werewolf* (2009), *The Clearing* (2010), and *Wherever You Go* (2011). Growing up in Seattle, Heather knew she'd be a storyteller. But after majoring in film at college, she abandoned a scholarship to a master's program in film in order to marry the first boy who said he loved her. Eight years later, she started writing novels and they saved her life.

GETTING STOOD UP

Daniel Ehrenhaft

Dear Teen Me,

Picture the scene: Your boarding school crush (we'll just leave it at that in order to protect her identity here) has asked you to see a movie in New York City. This is a big deal for all sorts of reasons. Even though they're arranged by your boarding school, shuttle bus trips to New York City suggest the possibility of something exciting and dangerous. So yeah, of course you're going to go. When you get into the city, you sign out to an exact location—a movie theater or a gallery or something like that...but the truth is that you only have two goals for the day: (1) find a hash pipe (even though you'll overpay for one and never use it), and (2) hook up with your Crush.

Your Crush is already in New York City visiting her family, so she's not on the shuttle bus. But you've arranged a meeting spot: a bodega off of Union Square, near the theater.

When you arrive, she's not there.

You circle the block, hoping there was some misunderstanding. You're a boarding school kid, after all; New York City is full of secrets that only the locals know—so perhaps there's another bodega? Since ninth grade, you've always secretly imagined and identified yourself as a New York City kid precisely because *you go to boarding school*. All your new friends live in New York City. You might as well be a local...right? You've long since severed most ties you have with your hometown, except for one close friend and your immediate family. But now you feel terribly alone. There is no other bodega; there was no misunderstanding.

But there is a used bookstore. So you wander in—knowing you have hours to kill (there's no way you're going to see a movie alone), and knowing you'll have to come up with a fabulous lie to convince your friends she didn't blow you off (there's no way they'll believe you). Instead, you find a dog-eared copy of *Mother Night* by Kurt Vonnegut. You loved *Cat's Cradle* and *Slaughterhouse Five*, so you dive in. You get lost in it until it's time to board the shuttle bus home.

Years later, you'll try to justify this crushing disappointment as a "turning point." You'll try to attach cosmic significance to it. Ha! Pure BS. I can tell you so because I ran into your Crush recently. She claims that she had a huge crush on you, too. She claims she blew you off that day because she was worried you wouldn't show. She claims all sorts of things. Weak excuses, but you let them slide. You both laugh. Either way, your kids are the same age, just toddlers, so you arrange a playdate, knowing it will never happen. Neither of you can remember the movie you went to. You think it was *Sid & Nancy*. She thinks it was *A Fish Called Wanda*.

Doesn't matter. Because you know what? You suddenly felt much lighter.

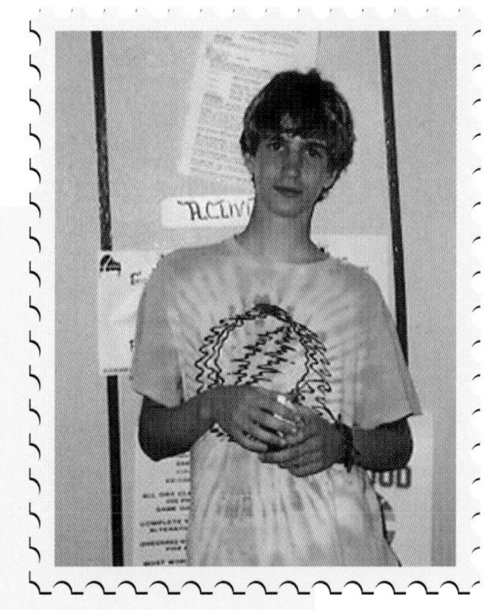

Daniel Ehrenhaft is the author of far too many books for children and young adults. He has often written under the pseudonym Daniel Parker (his middle name, which is easier to spell and pronounce than his last), and occasionally Erin Haft. He lives in Brooklyn with his wife, Jessica; their son, Nate; their scruffy dog, Gibby; and their psychotic cat, Bootsy. When he isn't writing, Mr. Ehrenhaft is the editorial director of Soho Teen, at Soho Press. As evidenced from the photo at right, he has been a musician since the late 1970s, and he is a member of Tiger Beat, the only YA author band on the planet. Other work experience includes a short term of employment at the Columbia University Library. He was fired.

LOSING YOUR SIGHT SHOULDN'T MEAN LOSING YOUR RIGHTS

Laura Ellen

Dear Teen Me,

There's no easy way to say this, so I'll just be blunt. The way you see—you know, with that sunspot-like-thing that blocks your central vision? That's not normal. In a few days you're going to go to the eye doctor and he's going to tell you that you have an eye disease called macular degeneration.

Okay, stop freaking out. It doesn't mean you're dying. But it does mean that you have a label now, "visually impaired," which will affect how others see you—and, unfortunately, how you see yourself.

I won't lie. Life is about to get really hard. At times it will downright suck, especially when you discover there are things others take for granted that you just can't do. Like drive, or read regular print, or see faces unless you're really close up (and even then you'll have to look at their ears to see their eyes). Weird, I know.

But seriously, who cares? Most of the people in New York don't drive, and there are audio books and magnifying glasses and ways to make print really big....It never gets easy staring at ears, and there's no surefire way to deal with the jerks who embarrass you by looking all around before asking, "Are you talking to me?" And yes, all of that stuff will make you feel flawed and "abnormal." But normal is boring. It's predictable and monotonous. "Different," though, different is cool and intriguing and way more fun.

Some of your teachers will try to pretend you see like everyone else, however—because being different means more work for them. They don't want to type their tests, because they're used to handwriting them at the last minute, and they don't want to print their lecture notes in advance, because they actually don't *have* any notes; they usually just wing it.

But try to understand: Their refusal to help has nothing to do with you. They're tired and overworked and set in their ways. They've lost sight of the fact that their job is to teach. They see your request for accommodations as annoying and time-consuming, rather than what it is—your only way to access the material.

Shake their behavior off. I promise, for the handful of rude and ignorant teachers that you'll have to deal with, there will be so many more who will go above and beyond for you—like the school nurse. She'll spend hours enlarging *Emma* and other novels for you on the school copier whenever a large-print version isn't available.

Like I said, don't let those other people stress you out—but don't stand for their ignorance either. You aren't being difficult. It's your *right* to ask for those accommodations. Don't sit red-faced and silent when that history teacher hands you an illegible, handwritten test for the twentieth time. Don't cower in the corner when that Spanish teacher writes the entire exam on the board and doesn't let you get out of your seat to read it.

Stand up for yourself.

I know, as shy and timid as you are, it's hard to imagine pushing back, but do it. If you don't, no one else will. Those teachers are banking on your passivity, so that they can continue to sit and be passive themselves. Don't let them get away with it. What those teachers are doing, or not doing, is wrong. And when they humiliate you in front of the class with their insensitive remarks, not only is that wrong, that's bullying. And it's not okay.

So...

Open your mouth.

Say something.

Refuse to accept it.

You're not a second-class citizen; don't let them treat you like one.

This whole thing is a lot to hear, and I'm sorry if it's a bit overwhelming, but I need to tell you a little more. As your eyes get worse and you find yourself battling ignorant, insensitive individuals on a daily basis, you're going to become angry and frustrated, and very, very confused. Everyone suddenly treats you differently, but you don't *feel* any different. This will make you wonder if they see someone else when they look at you. You'll start doubting yourself, hating yourself, and yes, you'll even contemplate ending your life.

Stop.

Take a breath.

Write.

Listen to music.

And then write some more.

You can do this. I promise.

I know you feel lost. You want to talk to someone about it, but you feel like your family and friends don't understand—and, well, they don't. But neither do you, right? This whole thing is new to everyone, and no one knows quite how to act or what to say or what to do. Don't let all that confusion stop you. Tell them how lost you feel. Let them help you.

And try not to trade your friends for those idiot boyfriends I can see creeping up. Once upon a time—okay, just a year before you were first diagnosed—you were interested in sweet, decent guys. But when your confidence began to plummet and you started doubting yourself, you left your friends behind and started gravitating toward losers.

I get it. I do. Things with your friends have gotten a little weird. You hate that they always have to drive you around and read the menu to you. You feel like you're a burden to them. Meanwhile, those guys make you feel wanted. Normal. And they never ask you any questions about your eyesight, which comes as a relief—even though your friends are only asking because they actually care (which is more than I can say about those guys). So instead of drowning yourself in the loser brigade and getting hung up on what you can't do, focus your energy on what you can do.

Stay away from the guy who acts like you have to be with him every waking moment (he cheats on you when you're out with your friends). Run from the guy who demeans you, insults you, and throws your eyesight in your face like it's something shameful that no one but him would ever put up with (that's emotional abuse—and he has no right to treat you like that). These guys know they don't deserve you, but they also know your eyesight has made you insecure and self-conscious—weaknesses that losers like them are looking to prey on. You're not a loser, so don't date guys who treat you like one. Having an eye disease doesn't make you any less of a human being.

And the other guy? The one that you think is so different from the others? I know how nice he seems—and he *is* nice. He doesn't call you names or put you down, and he always puts you first. But he's also using your eyesight as a crutch, as an excuse for his own shortcomings. Anytime he fails at something, he says it's because he has to help you. Because you're "disabled." You're not disabled, and you're not a fool. Walk away, girl. Just walk away.

You're a capable, strong, creative, and intelligent girl. You don't need some guy to define you. You need to define yourself. All this turmoil that you're about to go through—as unfair as it seems right now—is going to teach you to be self-reliant, confident, and strong. But most importantly, it's going to turn you into a survivor—and those survival skills are things that you can turn around and teach to others, too. And in the meantime, all that writing that you're doing right now (because you're the only one you can talk to who actually understands)—keep at it! It will actually turn into a career someday. Seriously, it will. So do what you want, be yourself, *love* yourself. Once you do, I promise, things will start to fall into place.

Stay strong.

P.S. *PLEASE* stop pretending you don't know the answers in math class! It's okay to be smarter than the boys. Really. They'll get over it.

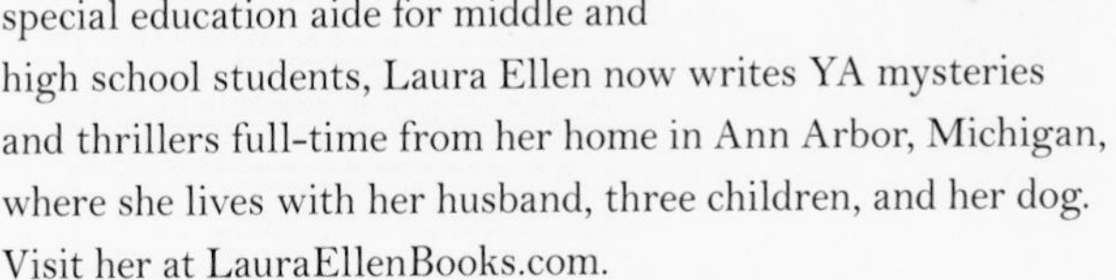

Laura Ellen used her experiences growing up with macular degeneration to add powerful authenticity to her debut thriller, *Blind Spot* (forthcoming), a suspenseful and emotional page-turner for teens. A former language arts teacher and special education aide for middle and high school students, Laura Ellen now writes YA mysteries and thrillers full-time from her home in Ann Arbor, Michigan, where she lives with her husband, three children, and her dog. Visit her at LauraEllenBooks.com.

I HOPE YOU DANCE—TO THE THEME FROM *BONANZA*

Beth Fantaskey

Dear Teen Me,

First of all, rest easy: Mom and Dad's prediction that you'll "burn the house down someday with that deep fryer" will never be realized. Of course, this is largely because your parents will ban you from ever using the deep fryer, after what you did to their kitchen. (Unfortunately, you'll never be the type of person who can be trusted with hot grease.)

Similarly—and this may disappoint you—you will always be weird and shy. While you'll eventually lose your unruly curls and adopt a trademark "pixie" cut, you can't snip away these traits, which are so central to your personality.

Right now you're worried about both your shyness and your weirdness. It's clear that you're never going to be a cheerleader or go to the big parties on the riverbank. And not only is it obvious that you'll never date a football star, but also, right now, you're worried that you'll never date *anyone*. Ever. (But don't worry: you will.)

And yet: You've got lots of great friends who are also on the margins, and there are moments when you see through the myth of "popularity" to realize that you secretly like your spot among the geeks, dweebs, and "arty" kids. There's the day Bonnie eloquently challenges your civics teacher's opinions on Keynesian economics, leaving everybody speechless. And the night when Sandra unveils a stack of records from an old jukebox, and you spend hours dancing to the theme from *Bonanza*. And there will also be a moment when one of your closest male friends finds enough courage and support to come out while you guys are all sitting around the campfire.

All this stuff—it leaves you conflicted. You're pretty sure that the popular teenagers don't have goofy dance parties to crazy old records—I mean, they usually just hang out by the river, drinking. And "normal" teenagers don't like economic theory, or—heaven forbid in rural Pennsylvania in 1984—"come out." Yet you like your small group of friends and the things you do together. They get your offbeat sense of humor and don't make fun of you when you decide to wear thermal underwear as leggings one day, or that you quit tennis because the whole idea of hitting a ball for hours just leaves you feeling...*eh*.

Go ahead and embrace life on the social fringes, because one day you'll realize—without a doubt—that it's where you *want* to be. You'll reject all accepted definitions of what's "cool" and actively seek out friends who see the world a little...differently. You'll even marry one of those weirdos—and it'll be great. You're going to laugh. A lot.

And that weirdness inside of you—the quirkiness that compels you and your best friend to speak French constantly throughout your junior year—is going to have a more immediate payoff too, because your teacher will note your strange habit and help both of you win scholarships to spend the next summer at a university in France. That experience—living on a foreign campus at age sixteen—will ignite a lifelong passion for travel that will take you around the globe. You will never have the attention span needed to safely operate a deep fryer, but you'll confidently navigate life in places like China, India, and Eastern Europe. That's not bad, right?

So best wishes, be true to your inner geek—and expect to have a truly "bon voyage!"

In spite of not having a date to the senior prom, **Beth Fantaskey** went on to live a happy life in Lewisburg, Pennsylvania, with her husband, Dave; their three daughters; and a fish named PrimeTime. She is the author of *Jessica's Guide to Dating on the Dark Side* (2009), *Jekel Loves Hyde* (2010), and *Jessica Rules the Dark Side* (2011), all published by Houghton Mifflin Harcourt.

JEKYLL & HYDE

Caridad Ferrer

Dear Teen Me,

You've got a bad case of the Jekyll and Hydes. I mean, *sans* the whole split-personality thing, it pretty much nails you, doesn't it? C'mon, let's examine the evidence.

There's the side that's crazy shy (let's refer to this as the Jekyll half) and born into a family that Just Doesn't Get It. They don't even *know* how to spell shy. Your dad is the life of the party; your mother is a natural attention (read: "man") magnet; your brother could sell ice to an Eskimo, and your sister's idea of a good time is going into a room where she doesn't know a single soul. And that's just your immediate family. The rest of the relatives? They aren't any better, most of them falling under some variation on a theme of Extreme Extrovert.

Pfft.

To you, shoving bamboo shoots under your fingernails sounds like a better alternative to small talk.

So to say they don't understand what you mean when you say you're feeling shy is putting it mildly. They think it's a silly pretense, especially when you balk at being paraded in public like a trained monkey, playing the Bach Invention that won you that piano competition or reciting the poem that your fifth-grade teacher insisted on entering in the Dade County Youth Fair, and which won first place. Which brings us to the second reason why they have a hard time understanding your reactions. After all, why on earth do you enter competitions if you don't *want* the attention, right?

Which brings us to Hyde. *That* side of your personality is as competitive as Jekyll is shy. But explaining that you love competition—that you love competing against yourself as much as you love competing against others—is usually met with blank stares. They don't get that you're simply incapable of taking on a pursuit if you don't intend to become the best you personally can. Which has the unexpected side benefit of allowing you to fake it—people will think you're totally outgoing and confident.

No wonder people don't get it. You hardly get it yourself.

On the one hand you've got Hyde saying, "Come *on*, dude. Those people out there—they're not doing *anything* you can't do. Let's go!" while Jekyll's all, "Oh, I don't know, it's getting pretty crazy out there, isn't it? Hey, look—a nice dark corner!"

Welcome to the battle you're going to wage for the rest of your life. The Jekyll in you will pull away from the spotlight, so scared of being made a fool of that you'll work yourself into an anxious, stomach-churning lather, while your Hyde side will force you to overcome the nausea and just get on with it, already. Jekyll's going to win for a long time—the anxiety will rise to levels such that you'll abandon a lot of your dreams, finding it easier to retreat and blend into the wallpaper, even as Hyde writhes inside you, furious that you're such a monumental wuss.

Don't look at it as being a wuss—look at it as...hibernation. Because I promise, there will come a time when you'll bust out, voluntarily, in full, glorious Technicolor. You'll be an engaging (or so you've been told) presence on panels, win prestigious writing awards before your peers, and even step out onto a competitive ballroom dance floor.

And Hyde'll be right there, helping you enjoy the spotlight.

Caridad Ferrer

Caridad Ferrer is a first-generation Cuban-American, whose YA debut, *Adiós to My Old Life*, was a Romance Writers of America's 2007 RITA winner and was named to the 2009 Popular Paperbacks for Young Adults list, awarded by the American Library Association. Her latest young adult novel, *When the Stars Go Blue*, a contemporary retelling of Bizet's *Carmen*, was recently honored as the first-place YA Novel: English Language at the 2011 International Latino Book Awards.

BE HONEST WITH YOURSELF

Michael Griffo

Dear Teen Me,

At some moments it seems like it truly has been thirty years since I was in high school. But at other times I can still hear the late bell ringing and the locker doors slamming shut. It's like I'm still there with you, like a part of me has never let go.

So much happened during those four years, but the most rewarding and life-changing experience occurred when you were cast in the school play. Do you remember how quickly you made new friends, gained respect from your teachers, and learned that you loved being onstage? It was also the first time you fell in love.

I wonder: Was it really Love, with a capital *L*? I'm still not sure, but it was the first time you thought about wanting to kiss another person. The first time your palms got sweaty when you were standing next to someone else. And the first time you were forced to admit that these "firsts" were happening because of another guy.

I don't even remember his name. Can you believe that!? But I can see his face so clearly it's as if I'm back onstage, dressed as Barnaby Tucker in the musical *Hello, Dolly!* and he's standing right next to me dressed in a brown plaid wool suit, his curly blonde hair spilling out from underneath his cap, as we're about to perform the song "Femininity." (Isn't that an ironic title?!)

During the song, you had to do a barrel roll over this guy's back and then jump back on top of him. You were short and he was quite tall and muscular and you loved the view of the world when you were holding onto his shoulders. And you never wanted to let go. You developed a powerful crush on him. So powerful and eye-opening that you never told another soul. You kept silent simply because you were too embarrassed and ashamed. And when he would smile at you and ask how you were doing, you would lie and say that you were fine.

This started you on a long and successful career of lying. Of keeping the truth about yourself hidden. You kept the fact that you were gay a secret for a very long time and it stunted your emotional growth. You had no idea how to form an honest, adult relationship, because you couldn't form an honest relationship with yourself. And you didn't know how to act with other guys because you never took chances. I don't think you should have professed your undying love to your onstage partner, but you definitely should have looked yourself in the mirror and been honest. You should have told yourself that these feelings you had were real. And you should have confided in your parents, or talked with Rob or Don—your closest friends—and asked them to share some of the burden that you were carrying; that's what family and friends are there for. You shouldn't have tried to do it on your own.

So Michael, if you're listening, don't spend time living your life in a vacuum. Reach out to someone you can trust—a parent, a teacher, a friend—and tell them what's going on inside your brain and your heart. Don't worry about how they'll react; they may be surprised, and they may not understand, but at least they'll know.

Which means that no matter what, you won't ever be alone again.

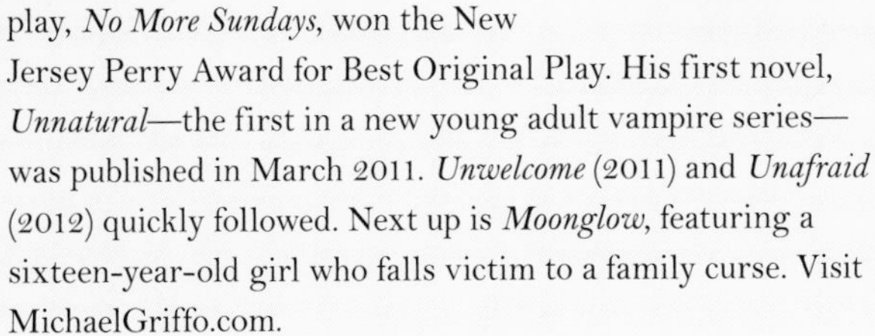

Michael Griffo performed as an actor throughout the country, off Broadway, and as far away as Hong Kong. He made the transition to playwright in 2001 and his first play, *No More Sundays*, won the New Jersey Perry Award for Best Original Play. His first novel, *Unnatural*—the first in a new young adult vampire series—was published in March 2011. *Unwelcome* (2011) and *Unafraid* (2012) quickly followed. Next up is *Moonglow*, featuring a sixteen-year-old girl who falls victim to a family curse. Visit MichaelGriffo.com.

THE SKINNY GIRL

Janet Gurtler

Dear Teen Me,

It's kind of a rush isn't it—how thin you've become? It started with that boy you'd been crushing on. Your best friend asked him what he thought of you, and in response he reversed the words from the punk rock song by the Monks you all loved so much: Instead of "Nice legs. Shame about her face," he sang, "Nice face. Shame about her legs."

Wow! That comment hurt so much you couldn't breathe for a minute, and a shamed blush stained your cheeks. You hated being the chubby one in a family full of thin kids, and suspected that your size made you inadequate in some way. Teasing sucked, but this was different. This was from a boy you liked. And it was devastating to your already fragile ego. So a diet followed and the weight dropped off.

And for the first time now you're actually skinny. What a trip! You feel powerful, and really in control. I can see why it's hard to say no to the attention—the positive attention—that the weight loss gets you. You start hanging out with the popular girls again, as if thinness makes you worthy, but inside you feel empty. Physically and emotionally. They love how skinny you've become, though, all those thin girls. When one of them brags about fitting into a pair of your jeans you feel like you've made it. Like your thinness is something to be desired.

Unfortunately, taking it off isn't the hard part. Starving yourself is sustainable for a while, but it's hard to keep up. You're basing your worth on how many calories you consume. And so now, when you do eat, it's pure guilt. Which leads to binges, and more guilt. And then you're starving yourself again. You're caught up in a vicious cycle.

But then another skinny girl at school shares a secret with you: throwing up. You try it, but you're not very good at it. That makes you feel like even more of a failure, and the weight piles back on again, but I'm so happy now that you couldn't make yourself do it. It's a dangerous, dangerous way to live, and some people who do it wind up so malnourished that they can even die.

But take a look at yourself right now. You've got a lot more life in you, and if you look hard enough, you're going to find a person with strength and real tenacity.

Being skinny seems like a path to happiness, but it's not. Trust me. Hang in there. There's not one defining moment when it all changes, but gradually you'll come to believe that you're kind of okay. You're actually going to kind of rock at middle age (if you do say so yourself). It's a great time for you (and it's not as far off as you might think). Remember how you always felt like an old woman lived inside you? Well, you'll grow into your skin, just like you predicted. You'll worry about your weight on and off your whole life, but it won't define you. Not like it does now. In fact, you'll have a pretty good time. You'll have friends who value you for more than your size, and you'll accomplish things that have nothing to do with how you look.

Someday you're even going to meet a boy who thinks you're beautiful—even with no makeup and with some extra weight. You'll marry him. He's going to love you no matter how you look. Because of who you are.

Janet Gurtler is the author of contemporary YA novels, *I'm Not Her* (2011), *If I Tell* (2011), and *Who I Kissed* (forthcoming). Although she is chronologically (way) older, in many ways Janet will always be a sixteen-year-old girl. Visit her at JanetGurtler.com.

IT'S ABOUT TO GET WORSE

Kersten Hamilton

Dear Teen Me,

Some people say God doesn't allow us to see our futures because we wouldn't have the courage to face all that trouble and heartbreak if we saw it all at once—but I don't think that's true. The thing is, I know a secret that you're just beginning to learn, and this secret isn't just important for your dream of becoming a writer, it's also critical to your survival. So I'm going to give you a little peek into the days ahead.

It starts with that litter of puppies. They're three days old, and their mother is dead. Everyone says you should drown them because they're going to die anyway without a mama dog to feed them. That's what they say. You're thirteen, but you gave up listening to what people said years ago. You've learned to think for yourself. You don't trust adults.

Your mom left when you were six. She fell in love with a man who didn't want kids, and she chose him over you and your brothers and sister. You haven't seen or heard from her since you were seven.

Your dad is an amazing storyteller—very charismatic. He can convince anyone that he's completely, totally sane. He doesn't tell them about the "voice" that tells him when to quit each job he gets, when to sleep, when to eat, and when it's safe to walk down the street.

You've had it with death and loss and craziness. You decide you're not going to kill the innocent little puppies. Not going to let it happen. And that's a good choice, teen self. You'll save them all, and name the one you keep Shadrach (after they boy in the Bible who came through a fiery furnace and lived to tell about it). He's a yellow mutt with a black muzzle, and he'll repay you a thousand, thousand times for saving his life.

Before Shad's a year old, the "voice" will tell your dad to stop talking to you. You'll have to make all your own decisions from that moment on, and you'll make some bad ones. You'll drop out of high school after your freshman year. Really bad choice. And because you're not in school, no one will notice when you disappear.

The "voice" says the world is going to end and demands that the family get off the grid before it does. You'll spend the rest of your teen years moving from one hiding place to another. You'll live in shacks and abandoned houses. And you will be so, so isolated (i.e., you'll have absolutely no human contact outside of your immediate family). Your dad still refuses to speak to you. It's only because of Shad that your heart doesn't wither and die. You'll love Shad, and he'll love you, no matter what.

Listen: As soon as your brothers are old enough to look after themselves, you need to get out of there. Things are different for girls in your family. Run. Wherever you wind up going, it will be good to have Shad with you.

And when you eventually meet your mother—try to understand that she is as broken as your dad. It wasn't anything you did or said when you were seven that made her leave.

The fact is, we can't know what the future holds, *because it doesn't exist yet*—it doesn't exist until we create it. No matter where you start, and no matter where you are today, you can dream a new tomorrow. Your parents can't stop you. You can create it through the choices you make (like the choice to save a puppy). If you have no adult to trust as a child, choose to become an adult that children can trust.

Kersten Hamilton

Kersten Hamilton is the author of *Tyger Tyger* (2010) and *In the Forests of the Night* (2011), both published by Houghton Mifflin Harcourt. She set about creating her future when she was thirteen years old, and Kersten managed to make more good decisions than bad decisions along the way. She's still dreaming a new and wonderful future into existence.

GOING ALL THE WAY

Bethany Hegedus

Dear Teen Me,

You stare at the neon green light on your bedside digital clock. In a few more minutes, you'll let Drew go—like, *all the way.* You've made up your mind. That's why you're here in the middle of the night. That's why you let Drew's best friend, Nate, pick you up after you snuck out of bed, crept down the stairs to the kitchen, and out the garage door. Not the big garage door with its electronic switch, but the side door that opens to the backyard—to where your family's golden retrievers sleep. Both Rainy and Snowy bark at you, and at that point you almost head back inside. Almost. Instead you run. You run for the corner.

When Nate picks you up, you don't know what to say. He's your friend. You've known him for the two years you've been dating Drew on and off. You don't go to the same high school anymore. (Zoning.) Nate plays saxophone in the marching band. Drew plays trumpet.

Nate fiddles with the car radio and mentions that Drew's car is in the shop. You make small talk. *Uncomfortable* small talk. Your best friend, Andrea, dated Nate for a few weeks. They broke up when she wouldn't give him a BJ. Dad thinks black guys are only after one thing—sex—but you know that's not true. You and Drew have been dating for a long time. You make out. You touch one another. But you've never gone all the way. He hasn't threatened to break up with you if you don't.

Tonight is the night—you know it.

You're in his bedroom. Drew nuzzles your ear. You've been kissing for what feels like hours. The bed creaks and your bodies shift. Your journal is filled with poems about Drew. About how Drew feels about you. About how hard it is to date a black guy. To deal with the stares of people in the mall. Or the movies. Not that you guys go out very often. Neither of you likes the stares.

Your friend Alicia lives in the same neighborhood as Drew. Her dad is a colonel in the army. Drew's dad is in the army, too, but you haven't ever met him. Before Drew turned the lights off, you saw his family picture. His mom, his dad, his little sister. *Why haven't you met any of them? Is Drew ashamed of you? Of your whiteness?*

You stare at the clock. The deadline has passed. You've been doing that all night. Adding five more minutes—working up your nerve. You're ready to go all the way. You're about to whisper, "I love you, Drew," when he shifts his body. He rolls away from you, pulls up his jeans, zips his zipper. "You better go. It's getting late."

You pull down your skirt, slide back into your bra. You stand like strangers in the dark.

Drew never knew that you wanted him to be your first. Five days later, you find out he's started seeing someone else. A girl who goes to his high school.

A few years later, when you do go all the way, it's a joint decision—something that's spoken about beforehand and attempted over and over again. (Who knew losing your virginity would take more than one try?) And when it does happen, no one's best friend picks you up. You drive yourself there and you drive yourself back home. And looking back, you're gloriously relieved that your decision wasn't dictated by the flashing of a bedside clock, but by your own internal clock instead.

Bethany Hegedus is the author of *Between Us Baxters* (2009), *Truth with a Capital T* (2010), and the forthcoming *Grandfather Gandhi*. She serves as editor for the YA section of the popular literary journal *Hunger Mountain*. A longtime resident of New York, she now lives in Austin, Texas.

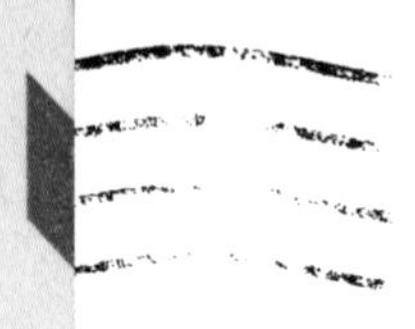

YOU ARE THE ELECTRIC BOOGALOO

Geoff Herbach

Dear Teen Me,

Humiliation and hilarity are closely linked, my little friend. Don't lie there in bed, your guts churning, as you replay the terrible scene. I'm *glad* your shirt stuck to the floor.

I love your break-dancing crew, okay? You and your friends from the rural Wisconsin hills have that K-Tel how-to album (including posters and diagrams). You pop. You worm. You spin on your backs. You windmill. In fact, you're not even that bad!

I love your silver "butterfly" pants (with forty-six zippers) that burst red fabric when you spin. Beautiful.

I love it when you take your giant piece of cardboard (mobile dance floor) down to the corner of Kase Street and Highway 81 to dance for traffic. Maybe you're right. Maybe a talent scout will be driving between Stitzer and Hazel Green. Maybe you *will* be discovered...Keep at it!

I love it that you have the guts to go into Kennedy Mall in Dubuque, Iowa to dance across from Hot Sam's Pretzels. You and your buddies go for broke in front of a small, glum crowd (who all eat Hot Sam's pretzels), and when security comes to escort you out, you scream, "Dancing is not a crime!" I love that.

I especially love what happened at Dubuque's Five Flags Center a few months later. You and your crew (Breakin Fixation) challenged Dubuque's 4+1 Crew to a dance-off. You practiced. You got T-shirts with your crew name emblazoned on them. You worked hard, and you daydreamed harder. You imagined the roaring crowd lifting you onto their shoulders. You didn't expect the Five Flags floor to be so sticky. You didn't expect to sweat through your new shirt. You didn't expect the flesh of your back to be gripped and twisted so that it felt like it was on fire. You didn't expect it, but that's how it was, and it hurt so bad that instead of spinning into a windmill—the main part of your routine—you just writhed on the floor, howling.

So okay, sure, people laughed at you—and you know why? Because you looked really funny.

Don't stay awake worrying about it, though. Don't wonder what you should have done differently. Don't beat yourself up, gut boiling with embarrassment. Don't imagine punching out the members of 4+1—you can't blame them for wearing slick Adidas tracksuits that didn't grip the floor. Just go to sleep, kid, and get ready for the next dance. It's all going to be great, okay?

How do I know?

Because now, so many years later, you can barely remember your victories (although there were some). What you think about now are the high-wire acts, the epic falls, and the punishing jeers of your classmates. You think about how excellent it is that you got up, dusted yourself off, and with utter seriousness of purpose, tried again.

Your immense dorkiness as a teen will be the center of your artistic life, the center of your sense of humor, the center of ongoing friendships with so many of the kids you knew back then. (You guys never discuss the relatively boring victories—you only talk about the grand, majestic, hilarious failures.)

What if you hit it big at that contest? Would you be a professional break-dancer now? Would success have gone to your head? Or would you be a rich banker? Or a lawyer? Terrible!

But instead, you stuck to that floor, with your back on fire with the pain, and you screamed.

Don't beat yourself up over it, okay? Just relax. Keep dancing by the highway, you splendid little dork.

Geoff Herbach is the author of two young adult books, *Stupid Fast* (2011) and *Nothing Special* (2012). He teaches at Minnesota State, Mankato, where he lives in the woods in a log cabin, like Laura Ingalls Wilder (except with air-conditioning and a nice gas fireplace).

NO CALLS FROM SPIELBERG YET

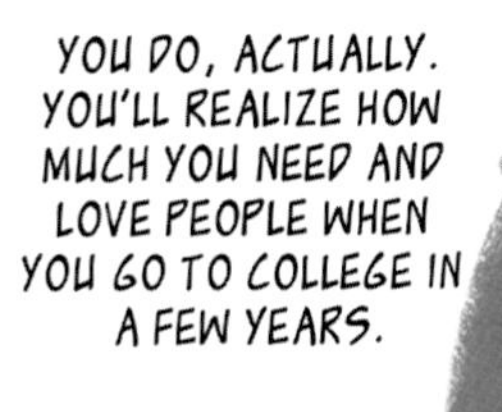

I KNOW HOW HARD IT IS TO SEE ANYTHING PAST HIGH SCHOOL LONELINESS AND MONOTONY.

BUT YOU'LL LEARN HOW TO TALK TO PEOPLE. YOU'LL LEARN HOW TO MOVE PAST YOUR SHYNESS AND MAKE YOUR FRIENDS LAUGH AND HOW TO LAUGH WITH THEM.

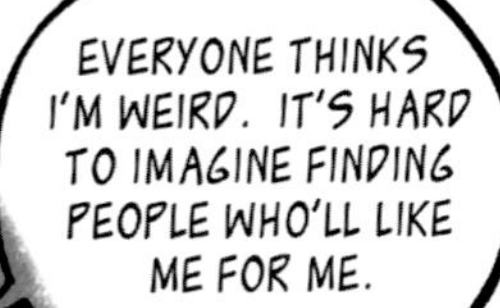

BOYS? OH, YOU'LL BE TERRIBLE WITH THEM FOR MANY YEARS. MUCH REJECTION.
GREAT.
BUT IT WORKS OUT OKAY IN THE END. YOU GET THE BOY WHO MATTERS, EVEN IF IT SEEMS LIKE IT TAKES FOREVER.
WHAT ABOUT BECOMING A WRITER? WILL I WRITE MY BOOK SERIES? WILL I HANG OUT WITH STEVEN SPIELBERG?
SORRY, NO CALLS FROM SPIELBERG YET.
DARNIT.
YOU STILL BECOME A CREATOR AND A WRITER, BUT INSTEAD OF NOVELS, YOU'LL WRITE AND DRAW COMICS BOOKS.
COMIC BOOKS? LIKE X-MEN?

Faith Erin Hicks has written and drawn thousands of pages of comics, some published, some online. Her previous work includes *Zombies Calling* (2007), *The War at Ellsmere* (2008), *Brian Camp* (art only, 2010), and *Friends with Boys* (2012). She can be found online at FaithErinHicks.com.

WHEN DANCE WAS YOUR WORLD

Nancy Holder

Dear Teen Me,

Excuse me for interrupting you while you're hard at work. In the picture I'm looking at, in the moment I'm thinking of, you're choreographing a piece to "Lady Jane," by the Rolling Stones. You've organized your dancers into three groups, weaving them in and out of the intricate threads of guitar and harpsichord and dulcimer. Every time you work on the piece you can't catch your breath. You're nervous and exhilarated and you wonder if you're crazy because getting this right means so much to you; you feel every note so deeply. The song sounds plaintive, sinister, and sexy all at the same time. You keep seeing Mick Jagger sneering as he gazes at some poor Tudor girl sobbing because he's dumping her. In your imagination, he looks like David Bowie as the Demon King in *Labyrinth*. Different rocker, same edge.

You are firmly convinced you have no edge. Though it's hard to believe here in the future, you're still very shy right now. You don't tell anyone how deeply that song moves you, especially since you're not totally sure what it's all about. But when you listen to it, you feel as if there's a world living and breathing inside the music. It seems like, in a way, the Stones *live* there, and that if you get the dancers to feel as much as you're feeling through the movements you give them, the Jaggerverse will shimmer into existence, and you'll suddenly find yourself living a Bohemian existence downtown.

Grossmont is your third high school. No one there knows that less than a year ago, you dropped out of your second high school and moved to Europe to become a classical ballet dancer—and that you came home six weeks later because your father died of a heart attack. When it happened your stepmother got you a ticket home—for the funeral, you thought. You fully expected to return to Europe to keep dancing, but your stepmother talked you into staying in California and finishing high school. Which seemed like the sensible thing to do at the time. But later on you find out that Mrs. Newman, your stateside ballet teacher, didn't think it was such a good idea. She felt like you'd lose your chance to become really good. But she never got the chance to speak to you before you got on the plane.

So after your dad died you stayed in America, but like Mrs. Newman, you worried that you had just killed your dancing career—because dancers start young, and they also stop young. Most dancing careers end by the time the dancers reach their mid-thirties.

Your stepmother moved your family to La Mesa, where you went to Grossmont, and that's where you are when this picture is taken. You've found a great studio, where you take every class you can, starting with the baby class and ending at nine at night. You come home from hours of practice so exhausted that you step into the shower in your leotard and tights, lean against the tile, and fall asleep. You stretch your legs over your head and hook your toes under the lip of your headboard and lie like that for hours.

And you keep listening, endlessly, to "Lady Jane," choreographing it in your head. And one day, your stepmother sees tears streaming down your face, and asks you why you're crying.

"It's the music. It's so beautiful," you say.

She gives you a classic *what the hell?* stare. What you have said is not computing in her mind.

"If it makes you cry," she asks, "why do you listen to it?"

She's genuinely bewildered, and you wonder if it's weird to cry when listening to beautiful music. You try to remember if anyone in ballet school in Germany cried like that. But in Germany, you guys were completely focused on your training, and afterward, those crazy kids spoke to each other in a language that was not English. You, being a Californian, opted for Spanish as your World Language (that is, before you dropped out of school). So as far as you know, no one in your *Balletthochschule* ever sobbed along to Brian Jones's dulcimer track.

In this time of uncertainty, your stepmother adds that dancers never make any money and they get injured all the time. She says that when the injuries are bad enough they end up teaching classes at the YMCA.

And so, in this picture of you at the gym, you are, frankly, falling apart. You're worried about getting injured and winding up at the YMCA (where you already have a job for the summer). You're stressing that you and your dancers won't be able to dance the Jaggerverse into reality, and you're worried that worrying about it means you're psycho. Because that *is* weird, right?

Then the coolest thing happens: a big, tall, muscular guy starts taking classes at your studio. He's a dance major in college and even though he's a modern dancer (not a ballet dancer, which you think is clearly superior), you two hook up. Yeah, he's a little older. But he gives you books to read and music to listen to and your stepmother is about to lose her mind because he's the closest thing around to Mick Jagger. That is to say, he's got a real edge. He tells you about this "project" he did where he danced around for a while wearing a raincoat, then climbed into a barrel while another dancer poured gallons of milk over his head and then added several boxes of cornflakes. You think this is a little bit random (okay, a lot), but the fact that he could even come up with something like this and, moreover, get the school to let him do it sends you soaring.

Plus, he partners you in classical ballet at the studio. You've never gotten to dance with a guy before, and it turns out that you totally light up the room when you leap into his arms and do a fish dive (sorry, that's the technical term) and then, after class, you two drive to Balboa Park and make out in the Organ Pavilion. (The unfortunate double entendre doesn't register at the time.) And your ballet teacher (Russian, strict, and, apparently, very romantic) tells you that you should marry this boy.

Which would be another way of dropping out of high school; but your man-dancer is not asking and, in fact, he leaves after a while because he's transferring to a new college.

So now you're losing the Cornflake King of the dance world, the only person you've ever told about your attempt to conjure the Jaggerverse into reality with smokin' choreography. And your heart aches when he makes his dramatic exit like someone in *The Black Swan.* You've always known in the back of your mind that he's older and that because you're so angsty and conflicted, you feel like you can't hold your own against a mature dancer like him. (Even if he is just a *modern* dancer.)

So here you are in the picture, your blood practically curdling with anxiety, and whatever I say to you right now will probably sound like a lecture. Except this: dance your dang fool heart out, girl. Because as of this writing, Mick Jagger is still alive, and so are you. Beautiful music makes you cry, and you know some great people who totally get that. And between this picture's now and the now of the future, you're going to conjure a lot of cool universes.

And, just for the record, I listened to "Lady Jane" thirty-two times in a row while writing you this letter. And it was amazing.

Nancy Holder

Nancy Holder is a multiple Bram Stoker Award–winning, *New York Times* best-selling author. The Wicked saga, one of her young adult dark fantasy series, was optioned by DreamWorks, and she has two other YA series: Crusade, and The Wolf Springs Chronicles. *Vanquished* and *Hot Blooded* will both be released in fall of 2012. She has also written lots of tie-in material for *Smallville, Buffy the Vampire Slayer,* and many other "universes." She received a Best Novel award from the International Association of Media Tie-in Writers for *Saving Grace: Tough Love* (2010), based on the TV show starring Holly Hunter.

LOIS LOWRY AND THE SPACE-TIME CONTINUUM VS. BOYS

K. A. Holt

Dear Teen Me,

Hi! It's your thirty-six-year-old self. What?! I know! (Good news: You finally have boobs. Bad news: That's not what I want to talk to you about.)

I want to tear your attention away from whatever poem you're writing, or world crisis you're trying to solve, and I want to address something more...personal.

I'm going to show you a list and see if you can figure out what the common ingredient is:

Writing. Books. Drinking coffee. Sleeping all day on Saturdays. Studying art. Trying to create a rip in the space-time continuum by figuring out the meaning of life. Listening to loud music. Going to plays. Making lists.

See what they have in common?

Yes.

That's right.

Those are all things you enjoy more than dating.

I just wanted to send you this note (although the technology that I used is a secret, trust me: It won't do any harm to the space-time continuum) to let you know that this is 100 percent completely okay. Just because you're a teenager doesn't mean you have to be boy-crazy. Your best friend might have a different boyfriend every two weeks and spend every spare second making out in the halls at school, but this doesn't mean you have to do the same thing. And I know it seems like every movie you see has a girl pining for a boy, but that doesn't mean you have to, too. I promise.

Boys can be great. You know that. They're funny and smart and nice to talk to. You like how their hands look, and sometimes you wonder what it would be like to sniff the backs of their necks. HOWEVER, this doesn't mean you need to say yes to any guy who asks to be your boyfriend. It doesn't mean you have to let boys put their hands all over you because "that's what teenagers do."

You don't have to date if you don't want to. Hang out with your friends, go to parties, but don't feel bad about those nights you want to lock yourself in your room with *Anastasia Krupnik*. (And even though I know that you think you're too old to be reading Lois Lowry, you're not—in fact, you *still* love Lois Lowry.)

Another thing—remember, I know your all your secrets—it's also absolutely okay if, when you're ready, you want to mix it up and date some girls, too. Just remember, the same rules apply. When you think no, say no. When you're not ready, say, "I'm not ready." And if you'd rather put on your headphones and read about Anastasia or Harriet the Spy or Scarlett O'Hara, you don't have to apologize.

There will be plenty of time for you to date. You have years to find your soul mate. Right now, though, I want you to concentrate on learning how to stand up for yourself. Do what you want, not what you think you *should* want. You'll figure it out. I promise.

Try to ignore all the pressure you feel to be a boy-crazy teen. Enjoy your quiet moments. Take time to listen to yourself. Then go for it.

Cool? Cool.

P.S. Boobs! OMG, I KNOW! FINALLY!

K. A. Holt is a mama, a terrible cook, and the author of *Mike Stellar: Nerves of Steel* (2009) and *Brains for Lunch: A Zombie Novel in Haiku?!* (2010). When she's not busy imagining how she would travel to Mars or survive a zombie apocalypse, she's busy imagining how she will survive the day. *Brains for Lunch* recently received a starred review in *Publishers Weekly* and was highlighted on the Texas Library Association's Annotated Lone Star Reading List for 2011. K. A. lives in Austin, Texas, with her husband and three children. None of them have been to Mars or are zombies. Yet.

SEEPING THROUGH THE CRACKS

P. J. Hoover

Dear Teen Me,

Isn't it cute how people call you "Trish the Dish?" Yes, it's totally flattering, and I'm glad you own it. If you're going to have a nickname, one that makes you out to be an attractive female is choice. I mean, it's way better than "phat." No matter how much explanation is given, that one never sounds good.

In case you don't know, I think you're fantastic. In lots of ways, I wish I were more like you. From your confidence to your intelligence (hello, math superstar!), and especially the way you plan for the future yet live for the moment, you're amazing. But here's the thing. You're letting something sneak in. Something you aren't even aware of. It's slipping in through the cracks, but it's like venom, and it's poisoning your mind. Here, from the future, it's so obvious, but you just don't see it. You never have. I wish I could make it stop, because, despite all the awesome things you accomplish in your life, this is the single thing that's caused you the most unhappiness and distress.

It starts small. Your dance instructor mentions you've gained ten pounds in the last year (puberty anyone?). A male classmate mentions some other girl has a nicer figure than you (obviously not a choice male specimen). Your pants fit a bit snug, and a "friend" feels inclined to mention this to you (le sigh. Why must people feel so inclined?). These little bits and pieces wedge their way into your psyche.

The first time you go on a true diet, you see success. You see how the less you put in your mouth, the more weight you lose. It's simple mathematics, and you've always been great at math. Remember, it's one of the things I love about you. So you start experimenting with eating, binging and purging and starving and compulsively exercising, and from there it's all downhill.

I wish I could give you better news. But the sad fact of the matter is that you plunge into a dark realm of anorexic and bulimic habits that stays in full swing for the better part of seven years. You try everything. First, you don't eat. Like anything. And yes, the weight comes off. But you almost pass out when you stand up, and you don't have the energy to walk up the stairs. This isn't sustainable, and you crumple. The forty pounds you just lost comes back, along with an extra ten.

The bulimia starts. And it stays. I'll be frank with you. You smell like vomit. Your face is puffy and swollen, and you're still overweight. And even though you think you are all sly and clever, everyone knows. You're not even fooling yourself. The years take their toll. Your confidence is crushed, and now you have a future filled with eating disorder baggage.

If you're looking for a solution, I don't have it. Even now, twenty-one years later, diets still make you uneasy. I wish I could tell you to get your head out of the toilet and listen to me, but you're too stubborn. Be strong. Find something to immerse yourself in. Maybe kung fu. Or Dungeons & Dragons. Look for a place where you don't constantly compare yourself to everyone else around you. Remember who you are. And remember why you are awesome. Someday the baggage will fade into the background.

P. J. (Tricia) Hoover writes fantasy and science fiction for kids and teens. A former electrical engineer, P. J. enjoys *Star Trek*, Rubik's Cubes, and kung fu. She lives in Austin, Texas, with her husband, two kids, a Yorkie, and a couple of tortoises. P. J. is the author of *Solstice* (2013), a YA dystopian-mythology story set in a global warming future.

FINDING YOUR VOICE

Ellen Hopkins

Dear Teen Me,

Your life was unusual from the start. You were adopted at birth. Your mother was forty-two when you were born, the "May" to your father's "December." He was seventy-two, and to put that into perspective, he was born in 1883. The son of German immigrants and the definition of a "self-made man," your dad parlayed a sixth-grade education into a couple of thriving businesses. He made his million dollars not long before he brought nine-day-old you home to a beautiful Spanish-style house in Palm Springs, California. Comedian Bob Hope lived next door and, having adopted a slew of kids himself, he sent his nanny over to help out for a few days. You were, of course, much too young to appreciate this. But let's just say that few enough people are given such an auspicious beginning.

The truth is, you were a child of privilege. Not so much because of money (though you never went without), but because of a very large measure of love infusing your childhood. You were doted on, and while your parents' age denied activities some families shared—skiing or mountain biking, for instance—your mom and dad rewarded you with things many children never have. You took piano and voice lessons. Studied dance—ballet, tap, jazz, even hula. You had dogs, cats, canaries, a lizard or two. You owned horses and rode fearlessly—barefoot, bare-headed, and bareback—across the desert and into the hills.

Your mother read to you every day, taught you to read on your own before you even started kindergarten. From her, you developed an ear for language and a passion for classic literature and poetry. Your father was no Puritan, but he wanted you to have faith, and made sure you went to church every Sunday. From him, you learned the value of honesty and hard work. A favorite saying of his stuck with you: *Anything worth doing is worth doing right.*

You went to a great private school, where creative teachers encouraged your talents. You excelled at academics, especially anything English or writing-related. You published a poem when you were just nine. Won trophies for your equestrian skills, ribbons at track meets. You aced piano recitals and dance competitions. By anyone's measure, these were successes. Yet, somehow, you grew up feeling...not good enough.

This probably took root in the knowledge that you were given away as a baby. Your parents were friends with the doctor who arranged the adoption. Curious about where you came from, when you were five you eavesdropped on one of their conversations and heard the doctor say, "Ellen isn't nearly as pretty as [her half-sister]." Later, you understood your birth mother was only sixteen, unmarried, and unequipped to parent. But as a small child, the message seemed clear: Not pretty enough equaled unworthy. Your birth mother kept her other daughter. She rejected you. You stashed that away, in a cabinet deep inside you, and there it will stay into adulthood.

Elementary school was your "chubby" phase. The kids would chant "Elsie the Cow," followed by a rousing chorus of moos. And though you shed those few extra pounds before seventh grade, the mirror will always reflect a fat girl. Not thin enough meant unlikeable. In a way, you denied yourself. The Guernsey goes into the internal cupboard, too.

So now you're a teen. Moving to a small town the summer before your eighth grade year means starting high school as the quintessential new kid. Just about everyone else here has been friends since kindergarten, but you don't know anyone. That puts you on the perimeter of some tightly closed circles, trying to push your way inside. Outsiders rarely reach "in crowd" status, and no matter how nice you are to the cheerleaders, you are no exception. Instead, you find acceptance among the intelligentsia, artistes, and anti-establishmentarians. In other words, the stoners.

And then, when you're sixteen, your father dies. Suddenly, you have to grow up very quickly, to help your mother deal with a funeral, probate, death taxes. You do everything you can to ease the process, but she falls into a deep depression, closes herself off from everyone, including you. You try your best to understand why, and on some level, you do. But it's yet another rebuff, and this time, from the person you're closest to.

So maybe it isn't surprising that you look to boys for approval. Not that you're easy. Your Lutheran upbringing has given you a solid moral compass. You're not interested in casual sex. What you want is someone who loves you. Someone who makes you feel like you are the most special girl in the world. You definitely connect with a few guys, but high school romances tend to be short-lived. With each breakup, you leak a little more self-esteem.

To sum it up, teen Ellen, this is how you see yourself:

Smart. Pretty much geek-smart, and who wants to hang out with a geek?

Plain. You'll never be pretty, so why bother with makeup? It can't hide the big bump in your nose. And forget about top-rung boyfriends. They're looking for glitzier girls.

Fat. The best part about that is not having to worry about cute clothes. Jeans and baggy T-shirts will do.

Decent at dance, choir, drama. To a degree. You don't get solos or leads. And you didn't make the cheer squad.

Different. You'll never fit into mainstream cliques. Plus, you have this annoying habit of making friends with other kids who are different, too. Which pushes you even closer toward freak distinction.

Probable yearbook description: Most Likely to Be Rejected.

Chin up. You won't know this for a very long time (when you reconnect with your old classmates through something called Facebook), but this is how other people see you:

Smart. Reliable. You're the one cheaters want to sit behind on test day. You'll ace your SATs and get into the college of your choice.

Pretty. You have a natural beauty that doesn't rely on makeup. Don't worry about your nose. No one notices it. They're looking at your smile.

Fit. Between dance, track, and horseback riding, you've got amazing legs and a great rear end. These are things no amount of dieting can achieve.

Talented. You continue to publish poetry and win every creative writing contest you enter. And you sure know how to rock 'n' roll.

Different. You are sensitive and more caring than most. You are a rebel, and speak your mind, especially about inequalities you see. You are brave.

Probable yearbook description: Most Likely to Take a Stand.

You graduate near the top of your class. Tossing that tasseled cap feels like the first step toward freedom. It is a sprint toward adulthood, where life will be just as confusing as ever. You'll drop out of college, choose the wrong guys. A couple will hurt you, and one will abuse you. Trust will come harder and harder. But each wrong turn makes you wiser. After a while you'll realize that love isn't about control. It's about mutual respect. Long-term relationships are born of friendship. And that has nothing to do with how you look, but rather who you are inside.

Eventually, you find forever connection with an amazing man. One who embraces you, and the responsibilities of a ready-made family. Yes, you'll have three children, one of whom will be responsible for an earthquake of pain. But you'll survive this heartbreak, too, and not only does it make you stronger, it puts you on the path you don't yet know you're searching for. (I'll give you a hint: Keep writing poetry.)

You will parent a fourth child, too. Full circle, you'll adopt him when you are forty-two, the exact same age your mother was when she adopted you. And, full circle, he will be bullied and struggle with feeling different. Being adopted has that effect. But you've been there, and recognize the emotions he experiences. You will help him grow into a brilliant young man, in part because of the things you have been through yourself. Your past helps create his future.

What I wish you could understand, teen me, is that the past *does* create the future. Everything that sets you apart also makes you unique. You are finding a distinctive voice, and one day that voice will speak not only *to* many, but also *for* many who can't speak for themselves. All that rejection helps you grow a thick skin, one you'll need when you finally settle into the career you were destined for. Being pushed away makes you want to gather others in. And you will, in ways small and immense.

Of course, if you suspected any of this now, you might just crawl into your closet and stay there, where it's private. Cozy. Safe. But here's the thing: Life isn't always safe. It isn't always happy or pretty or neat. Sometimes it's downright sad and ugly and messy. Dangerous, even. You have to take risks to discover courage. You must know pain to understand the true meaning of joy. And only through experiencing the sting of death will you come to cherish living.

You will make mistakes. Everyone does. Accept that—no, *value* that—and keep moving forward. I promise, in the future you'll look back and decide you wouldn't change a thing. Each misstep, each sidestep, each baby step brings you one step closer to where you belong, and once you reach this place, every day will bring immense satisfaction.

Dearest Teen Ellen. You *were* unusual from the start. Each inimitable day of your life helps create a voice completely your own.

Ellen Hopkins

Ellen Hopkins is a poet and the award-winning author of twenty nonfiction books for children and numerous *New York Times* best-selling young adult novels in verse: *Crank* (2004), *Glass* (2007), *Impulse* (2007), *Burned* (2008), *Identical* (2008), *Tricks* (2009), *Fallout* (2010), *Perfect* (2011), *Triangles* (2011), and *Tilt* (2012). Her first verse novel for adults, *Triangles*, was published in 2011. Ellen lives with her husband, teenage son, two German shepherds, one rescue cat, and two ponds (that's *ponds*, not pounds) of koi near Carson City, Nevada.

Q and A:

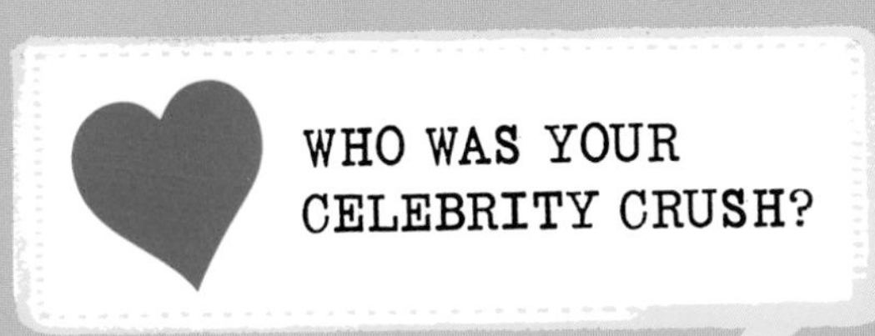

"On my bedroom walls, I had pictures of: John Lennon, Matthew McConaughey, Leonardo DiCaprio, Ani DiFranco, and Bob Dylan."

Elizabeth Miles

"Molly Ringwold–HUGE."

Geoff Herbach

"Brad Pitt. He also, coincidentally enough, went to my high school—twelve years before me."

Tera Lynn Childs

"The Beatles were first. Then Duran Duran and The Police. What can I say? I had a thing for pop rock bands. And it was the groups I obsessed over more than the individuals within them. I'm not sure what that reveals about me."

Jennifer Ziegler

"Fran Tarkington of the Minnesota Vikings."

Jenny Moss

"I was infatuated with 80's soul singer Terrence Trent Darby."

Bethany Hegedus

"Glenn Close."

Mariko Tamaki

~

"I didn't have one. I was too busy crushing on people in my immediate vicinity. I've always been practical that way."

Stacey Jay

~

"Johnny Depp from *21 Jump Street*."

Gretchen McNeil

~

"Patrick Duffy. I remember seeing him emerge from the ocean in *The Man from Atlantis*, and even though I wasn't ready to admit that I was gay, I knew that I was attracted to this man."

Michael Griffo

~

"Mark Hamill, a.k.a. Luke Skywalker."

Katherine Longshore

~

"They were all fictional. Laurie of *Little Women* and Aragorn of *The Lord of the Rings*. Carlton Buell from the Beany Malone books. Jed Wakeman in *Emily of Deep Valley*..."

Mitali Perkins

~

"David Bowie."

Mari Mancusi

~

"Jessica Rabbit."

Josh A. Cagan

~

"I had a thing for Judd Nelson's character in *The Breakfast Club*. He was witty and dangerous and smarter than everyone, though he was a total underachieving bad boy."

Amy Kathleen Ryan

~

"Harrison Ford as Indiana Jones."

Sara Zarr

~

"I guess it would have been Elizabeth Taylor—or maybe Annette Fabre, whom I fell in love with during grade school after seeing her in Disney movies—before she grew up in Beach Blanket Bingo. Something about girls—and women—with dark hair and soulful looks in their eyes attracted me more than the blondes most guys swooned over."

Joseph Bruchac

~

"Joni Mitchell."

Daniel Ehrenhaft

~

"Jordan Catalano. Does he count as a celebrity? I didn't even like Jared Leto, I just wanted to date Jordan Catalano. I had a thing for brooding, wounded birds."

Robin Benway

~

"John Cusack. And some things never change."

Beth Fantaskey

~

WHO NEEDS LUCK?

Stacey Jay

Dear Teen Me,

In the past few years, you've dated more than your fair share of creeps, and attended more than your fair share of funerals, and the road will only get bumpier from here on out. You are the opposite of lucky, my girl, so it's a good thing you have friends. Without them, you might not be around to write this letter.

You're seventeen and you're doing a LOT of dumb, dangerous things. Aside from drinking and drugging and driving your girlfriends to parties where you step over toothless addicts to get to the door, you have your own secret brand of crazy. You climb out on the roof and walk the ridge at night, letting your toes dangle off the edge. You have a stash of twenty-dollar bills under the ashtray in your car, and sometimes you get a few hundred miles into running away before you come back.

Sometimes you want to talk to an adult about how alienated and confused you feel, but you're afraid your parents and teachers and church leaders will hate you. You have a wonderful family, a solid community, and people who support your artsy-fartsy tendencies and think you've got potential, kid. You don't think you deserve to be so miserable.

But misery isn't something you have to earn. Misery is misery. It just is. I know what's going on inside of you, and...I wish I could say that you're not seeing things clearly, and that the world will be shiny and wonderful when you're grown up, but I can't, because it won't.

I can, however, offer hope.

In a few years, with the help of a liberal college staffed by amazing teachers, you're going to realize it's your society that's sick and twisted, not you. You're going to break free of the conditioning of your conservative, Southern Baptist childhood and declare yourself a feminist, an atheist (later an agnostic), and an independent. You're going to stop starving yourself to be "pretty;" you're going to teach yoga and volunteer and realize that parts of your spiritual upbringing were dead on—it *is* a blessing to serve others, and far better to give than to receive.

And the seeds for a self-destruction-free future are already being sown *right here, right now*, in the midst of all the craziness, and being protected by the most amazing support group you'll ever have, a fierce gang of guardians you completely take for granted. Because surely everyone has friends like these. Friends who stand up for you and *to* you and call you on your bullshit. Friends who stay up late talking about religion, politics, love, pain, and what it means to be human. Friends who enjoy the good times together, and get each other through tough times, too. Friends who drink hard but love harder; who stand together and protect each other and refuse to ever leave a friend behind.

Your friends save your life every day. Not only by taking care of you when you do stupid things, but by letting you take care of them. They're teaching you how to love and play and think for yourself. They're teaching you that kinship isn't only forged by blood. Slowly but surely, through the love they give, they're making up for all the luck you lack.

But who needs luck when you have such very good friends?

Years will pass and you'll fall out of touch with most of these girls, but you'll never forget them, and you'll wish every day that you could go back and give each one a tight hug and a big thank you.

So why don't you go do that now? Tell them it's from both of us.

Stacey Jay

Stacey Jay is the author of *Juliet Immortal* (2011) and *Romeo Redeemed* (2012) as well as several other books for young adults. She lives in Sonoma County, California, with her husband and two boys. Visit StaceyJay.com.

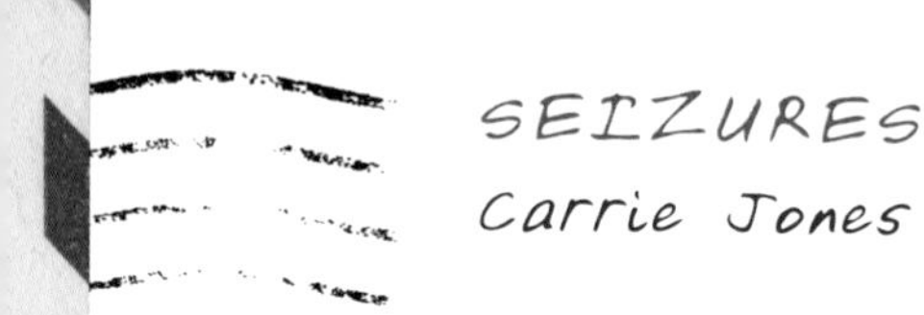

SEIZURES
Carrie Jones

Dear Teen Me,

Okay, a lot of people write about their health problems. And I get that. I mean, a lot of people like to talk about their broken bones and gastrointestinal issues, and whatever. That's fine. During flu season, people will go into graphic details about how they puked every two minutes. They'll even revel in details about the consistency of their vomit—and trust me, whether it was acidic or chunky, it was definitely gross.

You've never been one of those people, though. It's not that you think sickness shows some kind of bodily or spiritual weakness or something like that. You just think it's boring. And as far as you're concerned, there's nothing worse than being boring.

So when you were super little and broke your ankle playing tag at Debbie Muir's house, you didn't talk about it. And when you were in second grade and you broke your front tooth, you didn't talk about that either. You even kept your chronic bronchitis a secret.

And now?

I guess the older you—that is to say, me—is sticking to the plan. Because writing isn't talking, technically speaking. But I still feel this weird sort of apprehension, of nervousness. A little voice inside my head keeps telling me, "Sickness is boring. Tell a joke, Carrie. Tell a joke."

But seizure jokes are terrible, *evil* things. These are from Epilepsy.com:

> Do you know what to do if someone has a seizure in a swimming pool? *Throw in the laundry.*
>
> What's blue and doesn't fit. *A dead epileptic.*

There are some that are even worse, but I'm not going to include them here because I'm nice like that. So, you're probably wondering why I'm even telling you seizure jokes.

Well, in about a month, a boy is going to do something horrible to you. The incident and its aftermath will haunt you for a really long time, and it will affect your life in ways that you'll never expect. One of those unfortunate, life-changing consequences includes a case of mono—but, worse still, the virus that causes mono is going to act a little funny in your case. It's going to attack your brain. And it's going to give you seizures.

DO NOT FREAK OUT!!! Things I know:

1. You're about to go to college.

2. You don't have time for this.

3. You don't even like to talk about being sick—because being sick is boring.

And I'd like to be able to tell you that it's going to be okay. I wish that this letter could actually somehow reach back in time and grab hold of you there—so that you could avoid that party, so that you could escape being hurt by that boy, and so that you wouldn't have to suffer through seizures every day of your freshman year. But I can't tell you that. Things don't work that way.

Other things that are unpredictable:

1. Boys at parties.

2. Your friends at parties when your friends are wasted.

3. Seizures.

So, um, the points here are:

1. You're about to experience something truly awful. Even though you don't drink, a certain very cruel, very callous guy *is* drinking—and there's nothing I can do now to stop that thing from happening.

2. One of the lasting effects of this horrible experience is a virus that winds up giving you seizures.

3. Do not give up.

Seriously. That's the point. DO NOT GIVE UP. You're going to have seizures. You are actually going to develop a rash as a result of those seizures. The rash is pretty gross. Pack a lot of tights and pants to hide it. The seizures will start with your hand jerking. Then you'll pass out.

At one point you'll pass out when you're near a cute boy in your philosophy class. He'll try not to panic, but he'll also kind of fail. At another point you'll pass out in your dorm room. And once, you even wind up falling off a ladder at your *Othello* rehearsal. Sometimes you'll hit your head. Sometimes you'll wind up with so many bruises that people will think you're being abused.

Sometimes people will say, "Hey, aren't you the girl who has..."

They'll search for an inoffensive word. They'll usually find it. And you, for your part, will usually just be honest and answer yes. And a lot of those awesome people at Bates College won't care at all. They'll still love you despite the fact that you've lost IQ points from all the seizures.

Yes, Carrie, there will be cognitive degeneration. Yes, Carrie, that means you won't be able to recall recent conversations that well anymore, or class lectures, and you'll actually have to study.

Here's the thing: Your sickness isn't important. It's not going to define who you are. *You* have to be the one to do that.

Your first seizure will happen at home. You and Joe are hanging on the floor, watching *Amazon Women on the Moon*—this spoof movie that makes fun of other movies and shows. It's sort of a bunch of weird skits that feature things like a hero guy fighting against giant spiders, and a first lady who used to be a hooker. Stuff like that.

You aren't feeling great. You think it's the stress. A half-eaten tray of nachos rests on the heavy wooden coffee table in front of you. About four cans of Pepsi linger around the nachos, flip tops open, and almost drained.

"I'm going to miss you when you go," Joe says, in between bursts of laughter. He loves the scene where a bunch of naked women walk around doing completely normal things. It's his favorite scene in the movie.

"Yeah. Me too." You stop and correct yourself. "I mean, *I'm* going to miss *you*."

You scratch at the weird rash down by your ankle. It's a bizarre array of red dots and circles. It isn't bright; just sort of looks like faded markers. You hate it because it makes you imperfect. You also hate the idea of leaving Joe, even though you're super psyched about the future right now, and about getting out of the split-level house with the ugly brown couch. You're ready to leave the entire town of Bedford, New Hampshire, behind—because it seems to be nothing but rich people (except, that is, for you).

Joe is the "younger man"—which sounds pretty naughty, but isn't. He's a year behind you in school though, so you'll be going to college first.

And because it's one of the weaker scenes in the movie, and because, even though something awful happened at that party, you and Joe are hormonal monsters, you start to make out. Kissing Joe is like kissing sunlight. It energizes you, makes you all shaky inside, like you're doped up on a caffeine IV or something crazy like that. When you kiss him, you can smell him, and he smells clean, like white soap and Lubriderm moisturizer (which claims to be fragrance-free but totally smells). Your lips seem like they're magnetized, like they can't help but be drawn toward his, and everything is right in the world...until IT happens. You're inhaling that smell when he breaks away and says, "Your lips are kind of dry."

"Oh!" you grab for your Pepsi. "Sorry!"

You remember taking a sip...holding the can...hand shaking in this weird, rhythmical way...Joe grabbing the can, his eyes all soft and concerned...his voice sounding far away. "You okay?"

That's all you remember.

Bruce Link wrote, "Stigma exists when a person is identified by a label that sets that person apart and links that person to undesirable stereotypes that result in unfair treatment and discrimination."

The first step comes when people realize that others are different from themselves. They give those differences "labels." Next, culture determines that those people with certain characteristics are representative of everyone else who shares those characteristics, and a "negative stereotype" develops, which creates an "us vs. them" mentality. Finally, those who have been labeled begin to find themselves discriminated against.

There's a massive history of people feeling ashamed of their epilepsy. Epilepsy was hidden. Epilepsy was a secret. Epilepsy was something to fear. Epilepsy was and is a stigma.

But you have it, Carrie. You have it, and it will be okay.

Remember, we define ourselves. Define yourself as awesome.

Carrie Jones

Carrie Jones is the internationally (and *New York Times*) best-selling author of the Need series and other books. For more information about Carrie, please visit CarrieJonesBooks.com.

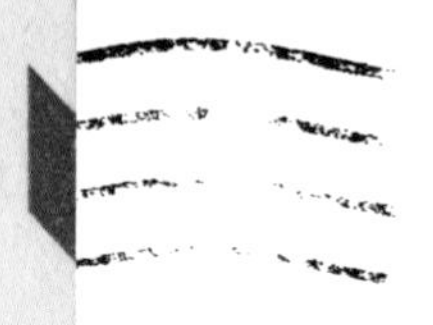

REGARDING YOUR COMMENDABLE DECISION TO LIVE

Mike Jung

Dear Teen Me,

It's good that I'm sending you a letter from here in the future, because I know it's not likely you'd trust me if I tried to talk to you in person. You don't trust many people, and honestly, why would you? You're fifteen, and fifteen, for you, was a monstrously bad year. Right now you can't even remember a time when your life wasn't all about bullies, bullies, bullies—they've verbally laid into you every day for the past four years, and it's gotten physical more than a few times as well. That's approximately a thousand days of hearing all the reasons why you're such a catastrophic loser: your face, clothes, skin, hair, lack of athletic ability, fondness for role-playing games, awkwardness with girls, bookworm tendencies, and ethnicity are all fair game.

It's also clear that no help is forthcoming. For example, there was that teacher who stood and watched through the locker room window as a cluster of bigger guys pushed you into a corner locker and showered you with racist, homophobic taunts, preventing you from getting dressed until the room was emptied out. And the fact that you're at least a year younger than everyone else in the room doesn't make things any easier—your suspicion that your parents were wrong about moving you up a grade is 192 percent confirmed.

Yep, good times. There are two years of high school left to go—you're looking at another 500 days of similar treatment—but the damage has already been done. The bullies and critics have convinced you that they're right.
You despise yourself.

I'm genuinely sorry. You're in emotional agony, you feel desperately alone, and you can't engage with the good things and amazing people that are actually there for you. In fact, fifteen is the age when you first truly consider the most extreme way out. Anger and bitterness—at your so-called peers, at your family, at the entire, unfeeling universe—nearly consume you, and in the years to come you'll spend more than one sleepless night deciding whether or not to go on living.

I get it, you know? You don't see any other solution. But there *is* another way—although it's a hard one. You can hang in there, deal with the loneliness and feelings of worthlessness as best you can, and wait it out. You want to get through this, my friend. I know it feels like things will never change, but they will (although in all honestly it's going to be a while longer).

You'll spend a long string of years coping with your rage, fleeing the black hole of depression, and struggling to make yourself whole again. You'll self-medicate. You won't date very many people, and when you do, your decision-making will be, um, questionable. And every time you see another human being, you'll instinctively turn away, because nearly every person on the planet looks like a slavering monster-in-waiting. But eventually you'll discover that the seeds of compassion, kindness, and generosity are still within you. It's very, very important that you keep those seeds alive, because later in life you'll finally learn how to make them grow.

It's not a given that those seeds of kindness will sprout, you know—in fact, there'll be times when you'll act in the same brutish, inexcusable manner as your tormenters. There'll be an incident later in your junior year involving a guy in your class who deals with some of the same treatment you do. The two of you have already spent a lot of time trying to humiliate each other, which is regrettable on so, so many levels, but one day you'll go too far. You'll circulate a questionnaire asking if this guy is the world's biggest...let's say *orifice*. It'll be a senseless, stupid act of cruelty, and while you might not deserve to be thrown headfirst into a wall (which is what'll happen—watch your head, chief), it won't be hard to understand the intensity of his reaction. The goose egg on your forehead will heal, but the loose thread in your moral fiber is probably still there to this day.

Thankfully, you won't go permanently down that road. That's not to say you lack a normal range of moronic tendencies, or that you'll never hurt anyone ever again, but after years of soul-searching and self-discovery it'll be possible to describe you as a decent guy. I know, "decent guy" lacks the high-school sizzle of things like "rock star," "babe magnet," or "party animal." You'll never morph into any of those things (although you'll occasionally humiliate the bejesus out of yourself in trying). It's easy to underestimate the value of being a decent guy, but it's what saves you in the end.

I'm not saying your future "oh hooray, I'm a decent guy" self-assessment will fix everything, because it won't. You feel broken at fifteen, and you'll still feel somewhat broken at my age. You'll still struggle in group situations, commit an atrocious variety of social blunders, and second-guess yourself on a continual basis. But you'll also understand who you are, accept who you are, and—miraculously—kinda sorta *like* who you are.

I know, you're thinking, "BUT HOW?" I'm afraid there won't be some clear-cut transformational moment when everything changes. What you'll do instead is retract your extremities like a turtle, and seek refuge in creativity—both other people's, and your own.

For example, there's music. Being a band geek isn't sufficient though, right? So instead, you become the first male flutist at your high school in what, twenty years? It's like writing, "PLEASE BEAT ME SENSELESS," on your forehead. However, every so often, someone tells you how much they respect that choice. At your age, it means *nothing* to hear that, but those little comments are piling up in your subconscious.

You'll keep making art, and for years that'll be your one reliable source of validation from the world. You'll copy down hundreds of superheroes, monsters, and other characters from pop culture, and then later on you'll create your own characters. You'll still occasionally hear about the Turtle Mafia decades later, for example—one friend will even remember that you came up with that *before Teenage Mutant Ninja Turtles*. More of those comments piling up, right?

You'll continue to submerge yourself in fantasy, science fiction, horror, and comic books galore. You'll *absorb* those books. You don't even know how much you're learning, but the incessant reading and drawing will become a thermonuclear source of internalized storytelling knowledge.

Eventually you'll hit this sweet spot where people actually want to hear your stories! It'll make all the difference. You'll always struggle to build relationships, but there are people you'll love, and who'll love you back. Sometimes it'll be complicated, or painful, or just plain weird, but other times it'll be *glorious*. On some days you'll feel the weight of life's cruelty and unfairness, and you'll shrug it off, because the different kinds of love you'll feel for so many people will propel you forward like psychological rocket fuel. You'll love your wife and children above all, but you'll also love the friends you make in all areas of life, especially in the world of children's literature. And your writing career will provide a slew of opportunities to express that love—which happens to be something you do better than almost anything else.

I won't press you to remember that time is on your side, because I enjoy the benefit of hindsight—time *was* on your side, though, and you made it! It seems miraculous, considering all the self-destructive choices you'll make just between the ages of fifteen and twenty-five. In a way, you *will* try to take your own life, but in a long, slow, downward-spiral sort of way. In the end, however, you'll choose to live. You'll finally realize you're not the waste of space so many people have said you were. Right now, you're laying a foundation for the rest of your life, and when you reach the place where I am now it'll feel like the world is absolutely exploding with possibilities. It's gonna be *amazing*!

Hang in there, pal. You'll be glad you did, and you won't be the only one.

Mike Jung is alive and well and living in Northern California—which is good because, you know, he likes it there. In a show of highly suspect judgment, his wife and two children live there with him. Mike's debut middle-grade novel, *Geeks, Girls and Secret Identities,* will be released in fall 2012.

GETTING PAST THE FEAR

Stasia Ward Kehoe

Dear Teen Me,

As I write this letter, you have kids of your own. I know, right now you're telling everyone that you're an artist, swearing that you'll never marry or have children. But there'll be a guy who changes that plan. Meanwhile, you'll bury yourself in dance and theater, pretending you're too busy for boys. Really, you're afraid of them. In fact, you're afraid of so many things that I sometimes wonder how you let your friend Aimee drag you to that frat party. It's probably because you were afraid to lose Aimee, who's one of your few reliable friends.

So now you're standing by the living room fireplace on Greek Row. The music pounds through the floorboards, and then up your legs and into your frantic heart. Even if Aimee hadn't disappeared into the crowd, there would still be no way for you to talk to anyone here. You stand still, afraid to even sip the punch (which smells more like acne medicine than fruit juice).

You're about to go sit out the rest of this miserable night on the front porch when Joe, the boy Aimee had come to flirt with, approaches you. He leans his arm against the chimney, shielding you from the frenzy. He says something about getting away from the chaos. You nod because you don't like crowds either, and Joe invites you to his room.

You want to get away from the party so badly that you actually think Joe's bedroom is preferable to the front stoop. And you justify your lapse in judgment by blaming Aimee for ditching you first. What you don't see now is that your biggest fear—even worse than boys—is of being lonely.

With barely a word, Joe leads you past the desk to his bed, directing you onto your back by pointing out the glow-in-the-dark stars on the ceiling. In the dim, quiet room, he starts kissing you. He tugs your tank top down, staring, while you feel about as romanced as a frog on a dissecting table. When Joe gets up, muttering, "I'll be right back," your brain finally kicks into gear. You fix your shirt, find the door, and run straight to Aimee's car. You're still there, shivering, when she turns up an hour later, saying that she never found Joe.

You tell Aimee that the party was lame. What you *don't* tell her is what actually happened—even though that might have saved her some heartache later on. Instead, you swallow the shame of that night, flashing back to the image of your exposed breasts, white in the fluorescent plastic starlight, again and again. You keep Aimee as your friend by nodding, agreeing, and keeping quiet for the rest of high school.

This is not the last time you'll make a bad judgment call. There will be other Joes. You'll spend several more years behind your angsty, artsy mask before you're able to openly admit how lonely and afraid you are.

You're going to find your way eventually, but if it were possible, I wish I could help you be more confident now. Have the courage to say yes to a year of study abroad, to say no to things you don't want. Ask for more time when you feel uncertain. Don't turn down a cool job because you're afraid of traveling alone across the city, and don't miss the opportunity to see a great show just because your friend bails. Your life is the sum of your experiences, and fear just gets in the way. So live more, and fear less!

Stasia Ward Kehoe is the author of *Audition* (2011), and she started dancing before kindergarten, writing before high school, and kissing (sadly) after that. She has worked in theaters, banks, computer labs, and publishing houses, and can name a cute boy she lusted after without taking action at every one of those places. She lives in western Washington with her husband and kids. Visit her at StasiaWardKehoe.com.

BAD GIRL

Tara Kelly

Dear Teen Me,

You meet her your freshman year. You're the awkward new kid who dresses like a goth one day and like your mother the next. She's the "school slut," the kind of girl every other girl warns you about. But she'll be the first person to reach out to you...the only person.

She's not the most beautiful girl you've ever seen, but everyone notices her. It's not her clothes. She dresses like a lot of girls, vintage jeans and baby tees with a logo or a slogan across the chest. It's not her sunshine hair or her scarlet lipstick. It's not even her voice, rough and sweet at the same time. It's the unconscious things, the little things. The way her lips are always turned up. The sway of her hips. The look in her eyes—she's seen enough life for someone twice her age.

The two of you always sneak off campus at lunch. Sometimes you go to the park. Sometimes her apartment. She talks about guys between drags of Marb Reds (the only brand to smoke, in her opinion). She's always dating some older guy...sometimes a lot older. You think it's pretty creepy, but you don't tell her so. She's not the first girl you've known who's dated older guys. And you don't want her to know how inexperienced you are. You don't want her to know a lot of things.

You wonder why she hangs out with you, why she doesn't see you for the dork you think you are. A big night for you is hanging out at the park with your best friend and his skater buddies, trying to get brain freeze from Slurpees. But your first night with her is something you'll never forget. Nothing major happens, but it's your first taste of her world—a world that will soon become yours.

She sends some guys to your house to pick you up while she gets ready. She only just met these guys the day before. They show up in this old muscle car. You won't remember the make or model...just that it was green and loud. She's dating the driver, who looks and dresses a lot like Spike in *Buffy The Vampire Slayer* (you'll see what I mean in a couple years). He likes his car and his metal at breakneck speeds. You think he's a lot older—old enough to buy

booze. Or maybe he just knows where to buy it. His friends are closer to your age, sixteen maybe.

You don't talk to them. They don't talk to you. The guy in the flannel keeps looking at you, though. Like he wants to say something. He's quieter than the others, a little less sure of himself. At some point he says, "It's okay, you know. We're not axe-murderers." You won't remember what anyone says for the rest of that night, but you'll always remember that. Don't ask me why.

You wonder how she does it. Never questions things. Never obsesses over what people think. She'll try anything once. You'll wish you could be like her. And sadly, you'll try to be.

Here's the thing: You're a freak. Always were. Always will be. You're a creative spirit who wants to bend the rules. But you're also practical and analytical. One day you'll love this about yourself. But right now you hate it. You just want to be free...like her.

But she's hiding as much as you are. One day she's going to show you who she really is...and it's going to terrify you.

I'm not going to tell you what happens, though. It's an experience you need to have. It's going to change the way you look at friendship for years to come.

Tara Kelly is a Jill of all trades—a YA author, one-girl band, and Web/graphic designer. She's written two YA books, *Harmonic Feedback* (2010) and *Amplified* (2011). Visit her at TheTaraTracks.com.

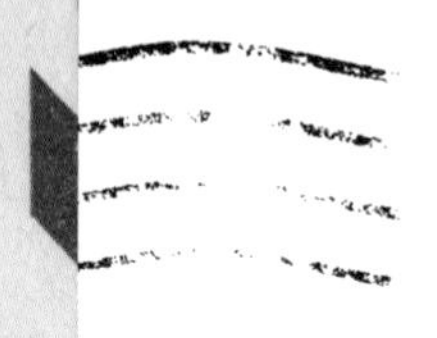

PICK UP THE PHONE AND CALL HIM BACK. RIGHT. NOW.

Miranda Kenneally

Dear Teen Me,

You've fallen for a guy you've known for pretty much your whole life.

Let's call him Charlie. He hugs you. He writes notes on the backs of your hands, using those orange and purple gel pens you love so much. He swaps sneakers with you. You laugh like crazy together, reciting lines from the Austin Powers movies. He always grabs a seat next to you in the church van.

Then he decides he likes your friend, and they start dating. You want to die.

He knows you love him, but he's just not into you like that. And he's the whole reason you decided to become a manager for the boys' soccer team! So now you're stuck with him every day at practice and at games. You can't stop looking at him, thinking about him.

You believe that if he doesn't start liking you back soon, you will die. For real.

Now for a bit of good news: There are some seriously hot senior guys on the soccer team—but every time they look your way, you bow your head and avoid them. You talk to the guys who are your age instead. You know you aren't pretty. You're nice and sweet and funny but guys don't like you. They like your friends. They ask you to put in a good word for them with Julie and Stephanie.

One day on the sidelines, the captain of the team—let's call him Jack—sits down beside you on the grass. He's eighteen and has this cropped brown hair and a nice smile. He's very cute in that all-American guy kind of way. Even in February, he has a tan. He's about to graduate.

You're fifteen. There's no way in hell a guy like this is into you, so you just act like yourself. You make him laugh. You tell him about this really cheesy pickup line you heard. "I may not be Fred Flintstone but I sure can make your bed rock."

He laughs.

"I saw your family in my church directory," you tell him. "But you never come to choir practice or to Sunday night socials or summer camp or anything."

"Yeah, I know."

"Why don't you?" you ask, just curious to know.

He adjusts his shin guard. Reties the laces on his cleats. "I dunno. I just haven't."

"You should come sometime. It's fun. This summer we're going on a choir tour to Florida and we're doing this mission trip thing, too."

Jack smiles at you.

The next Sunday, he comes to church. He hangs around with the preacher's son—the guy who plays quarterback for the football team—and some of the cheerleaders. And that's fine. He's very popular and in a different circle than you. But it makes you happy that he came.

Over the next several weeks, he keeps coming to church and you start telling him more about your life. You tell him about how much you like Charlie. Jack is sympathetic and listens to you whine about this other guy who is so not worth your time.

Right before he graduates, Jack writes a note in your yearbook. He tells you how much he's enjoyed getting to know you. That he thinks you're awesome. You show it off to your friends. "Can you believe he wrote that...*to me*?! Isn't he so hot?"

Your friends are most jealous, indeed. You read his inscription over and over.

Over the summer, he goes on the church mission trip with you. You're playing a game of poker after a day of painting an underprivileged family's home. You're practically in tears because Charlie has started hooking up with yet another girl, one he just met on this very mission trip. Jack tells you he doesn't know why you care about Charlie.

"You can do better," Jack says. "You're nice. You're honest and open."

You hear what he says, but you don't really listen to him. Miranda, you should be listening to this guy—this smart, nice, and thoughtful guy who keeps coming to your church events now that you've asked him to.

A few days after you get home from the mission trip, you're lying on your bed, staring at the ceiling. One hand rests on your phone. The other wipes tears from your face. All you want is for Charlie to call. To tell you that he was wrong; that he likes you, not her. None of your friends will listen to you talk about Charlie anymore, because they're sick to death of your obsession with him. You feel alone.

The phone rings. It's Jack.

"Hey," he says. "Want to come over to my house and swim? My parents aren't in town."

All you can think about is Charlie. What if he calls while you're at Jack's house? Cell phones aren't really mainstream yet. You don't have a pager.

"I can't," you tell him. "I don't feel well." Lie.

"Aw, come on. Come over."

You lie there, staring across the room at the pictures of you and Charlie that are pinned all over your bulletin board. You think about peeling off a T-shirt and shorts to reveal a two-piece bathing suit in front of Jack. It never has fit right. You're not skinny like the cheerleaders he hangs out with. Does he want to kiss you? What if he tries? No one's ever kissed you before. What if you're a terrible kisser because you've never had any practice? *There's no way in hell a guy like him would kiss me anyway*, you think.

You remember all the guys you've liked over the years. None of them have liked you back. A few boys have liked you, but you weren't interested in them. (You never gave them a chance. You were too worried that people would make fun of you for hanging around "dorky" guys.)

You don't bother to think about Jack's feelings because you assume that he, like everyone else (yourself excluded), lives a golden life. What if Jack needs a friend? What if he's lonely and looking for something and wants to tell you about it? Did you ever think that he started coming to church because you asked him to? Because he thought you cared enough about him to include him?

Why don't you ever think about anyone but yourself, Miranda? What if Jack needs *you*?

"I can't come over."

"Okay. Well, I'll talk to you later," Jack replies, and hangs up.

Now, over ten years later, I can tell you.

Jack never calls you again.

He goes on to college or wherever and you never see him again. Sometimes I look at pictures of him from high school and remember the series of conversations you had. In one photo from a soccer banquet, you're wearing a dress and he's in a button-down shirt and tie. He has his arm around you and you're both smiling. He treated you like a real person. He wasn't using you to get close to your friends. He just liked talking to you. And you screwed it all up because you thought he'd treat you like other guys had treated you.

Jack was right: You're honest. You're open. You take care of your friends. One day you'll look back on this time and wish you had listened to him.

You'll wish you'd picked up the phone and called him right back. "Yes, I'd love to go swimming with you."

I'm not saying that anything romantic would've happened. I doubt it would have. But you could've had a nice afternoon with a good friend. He might've invited you over again another day. He might've asked you to a movie. He might've asked you to go to Sonic for a cherry limeade, or to cruise around town in his truck or something.

You're in a great spot today, and you wouldn't trade it for anything. But the next time a great person tells you that you matter to them—listen to them. And then tell them why they matter to you, too.

Miranda Kenneally

Miranda Kenneally is the author of *Catching Jordan* (2011), a contemporary YA novel about football and femininity. Her other books include *Stealing Parker* (2012) and *Bad, Bad Thing* (2013). Miranda is the cocreator of Dear Teen Me. She enjoys reading and writing young adult literature, and loves *Star Trek*, music, sports, Mexican food, Twitter, coffee, and her husband. Visit her at MirandaKenneally.com.

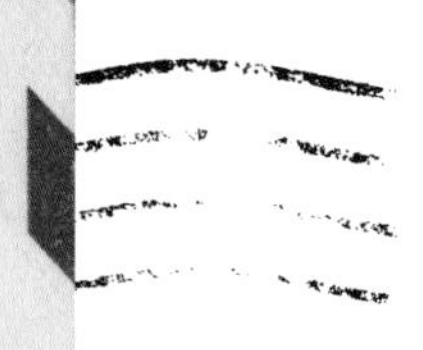

HE BROKE MORE THAN YOUR HEART

Stephanie Kuehnert

Dear Teen Me,

It started when he made you give Acacia that poor, pink, stuffed duck that he'd burned and stabbed and defaced with permanent marker with words like *Skunkhead*, which was supposed to insult Acacia because she'd bleached half of her black hair blond. "She's copying you," he said, referring to the blond streak you'd had in your hair for three months. You said you didn't see it that way, but he insisted, "She's jealous of you—of us being together. She's been spreading rumors about us."

You doubted this and you were right to. He cut you off from Acacia first for the simple reason that she was the biggest threat. If the two of you had stayed close, she would've noticed what he was doing to you. He said that she was out to get you. You believed him, because he was the first boy to tell you that he loved you.

He even said it before you did. You'd only been together for two weeks. It was earth-shattering. This gorgeous guy—a talented musician who looked like a dark-haired, hazel-eyed Kurt Cobain and smelled like sandalwood incense, cigarettes, and warm sheets—loved *you*, a girl who had just been used by two other gorgeous guys.

Of course if he really had been like Kurt Cobain, he would've joined you in trying to kick the convertible filled with loud, obnoxious jocks. They were screaming catcalls at you, but instead of supporting you, he threw you over his shoulder and lifted your skirt, flashing your underwear to the busy street. When you started to cry, he got pissed and said you couldn't take a joke. He also said your skirt was too short and those fishnet tights made you look like a slut. After a few more arguments like this, including one where he shredded your favorite shirt, you adopted a baggy, multilayered uniform.

You were all he had (he said), so when you did something to upset him, he told you he wanted to die. You did whatever you could to avoid this, including having sex with him when you didn't want to. He was your first, and the sex was beautiful...until that day he wanted to hook up in your friend Robin's garage. You knew she'd be mad, and she was the only friend you had left, so you said no and he gave you the silent treatment all day. Robin convinced him to talk to you and he said that if you didn't want to have sex with him anymore, it meant you didn't love him. So you did it. You never said no again, because you knew no one would ever love you like he did. He told you so.

After six months, he broke up with you anyway. You took a scalding shower and listened to Hole's cover of "He Hit Me (and It Felt like a Kiss)" a thousand times. Now it's dawning on you that even though he never physically hit you, he found other ways to smash you into a thousand pieces. You feel powerless, and blame yourself, and take it out on your own body with razor blades and alcohol. It will take you six months to call it "emotional abuse," and then a year to call it what it really was: "sexual abuse." It will take ten full years before you're ready to put it all behind you and love yourself again.

But you will, I promise.

Stephanie Kuehnert

Stephanie Kuehnert got her start writing bad poetry in junior high. Then she discovered punk rock and started producing DIY feminist zines in high school. She got her MFA in creative writing from Columbia College Chicago. Her first two young adult novels are *I Wanna Be Your Joey Ramone* (2008) and *Ballads of Suburbia* (2009). She writes about her teenage experiences for *Rookie* magazine at RookieMag.com. Visit her at StephanieKuehnert.com.

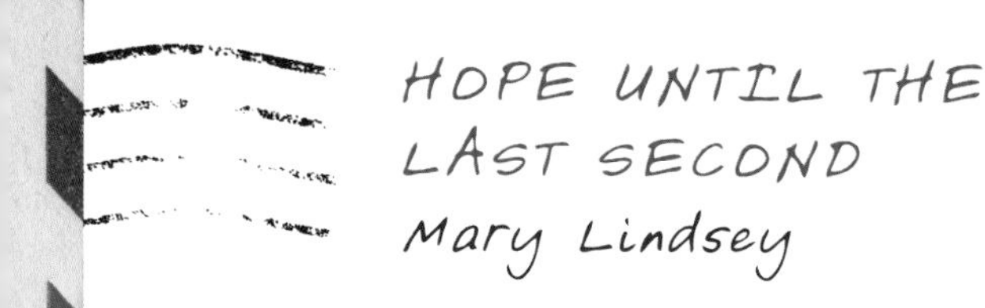

HOPE UNTIL THE LAST SECOND

Mary Lindsey

Dear Teen Me,

The adults around you love to say, "Life's not fair"—which is totally unnecessary. You're slapped in the face with that fact every time you step through the door to your house. Just like you, the house seems cheerful and composed from the outside, but inside, it's a disaster.

You use the trick you learned in acting class: Work from the inside out, and if that doesn't achieve the desired effect, cloak from the outside in.

I remember that last day of summer before your freshman year of high school. You made a pact with yourself. You closed the door to the laundry room (it was the only way to get away from *them*), and you vowed to never give in to addiction. You would not give up on yourself or on your future. You would never be like *them*, and you would never allow anyone to make you feel bad about yourself. Most of all, you'd never let anyone in on your private life outside of school. Success is based on appearances, and you would appear to be normal.

On one hand, this was a fantastic strategy. At sixteen, you'd realized that self-worth and outer impressions are keys to success. You have loads of friends (however superficial they may be) and will even be elected cheerleader—the pinnacle of high school success, right?

On the other hand, your strategy is unhealthy. You're lucky this plan worked, because holding things in is not only stressful, but it can be physically and psychologically dangerous.

Next year, when you're seventeen, you'll find someone with whom you can share your pain and struggle. Someone who will understand what you're going through and who won't judge you, gossip about you, or lord your secrets over you. Someone who will tell you that you can rise above it. Someone who believes in you unconditionally, and who will hold a place in your heart for the rest of your life.

Something else I wish you knew right now: There's always hope. At sixteen, you know in your heart that you will make it, but just as surely, you know that *they* will not.

The truth is, addiction can be beaten. Old patterns can be changed, and some of those people you are writing off as lost causes will turn it around, become sober, and pull away from the destructive behavior that you're trying so hard to avoid.

There's an old saying, "That which doesn't kill us, makes us stronger." It didn't kill you (obviously, since I'm here today writing this letter), and you're going to come out of your teens very, very strong. Hang in there. Your future will amaze you.

Mary T. Lindsey

Mary Lindsey lives in Houston with her husband, three kids, two dogs, her daughter's pet rats, an Australian bearded dragon, and dozens of Madagascar hissing cockroaches. She has taught drama and playwriting in a large public high school and English in a private school. It just so happens, one of the themes of her debut novel, *Shattered Souls* (2011), is the theme of this letter: There's always hope—even up to the very last second. Her second young adult novel, tentatively titled *Annabel* (forthcoming), is a gothic young adult novel based on Edgar Allan Poe's poem "Annabel Lee." You can find more about Mary Lindsey and her books on her website, MaryLindsey.com.

THE RAMIFICATIONS OF MOUTHING OFF TO CUTE BOYS
Nikki Loftin

Dear Teen Me,

I wish I could stop you.

I wish I could stop you from even sitting on that tree swing with your First Real High School Boyfriend (he's a sophomore and you're just a freshman!), Bill Underhill.* Because I see where this is going. And I really wish I could stop you from leaning in for that first kiss. (That atrocious, saliva-soaked, tongue-so-far-down-your-throat-you-gag-and-almost-throw-up-Lucky-Charms, poorly executed car wash of a French kiss.)

But mostly? I wish I could stop you from saying what you say about three kisses later.

When you ask—oh God—if he wouldn't mind NEVER kissing you like that again? Because he's a great boyfriend, but UGH! THAT WAS SO GROSS!

You know what's next: No more boyfriend.

You've pretty much always come right out and said what you thought, without thinking about the consequences. There are lots of times when it doesn't turn out all that great (although having your face exfoliated by Bill's tongue one more time would have been cause for homicide, so maybe you were right to insult the guy), but that runaway mouth of yours is going to cause real pain to friends and family members. Enough pain that I really, really wish I could get you to listen to this one piece of advice: Whether you intend to compliment or insult, think, for just a second, before you speak.

It's probably hopeless. Still, don't despair. Your tendency to blab's going to do some good, too.

For instance, in a month, your friends will start telling you how much the cute/popular Ray Vargas likes you. At the first high school dance, when he asks you to dance, you'll say yes, thrilled not to be the Utter Social Reject you were in middle school.

"So, you're cute," he'll say.

You'll giggle.

But then he'll say, "I hear you dated some real loser last year. Why would you do that?"

You have a sudden vision of the "loser" he means: that darling seventh-grade boy who brought you roses and made you a set of twelve-inch-tall initials—N.L.—out of scrap metal in shop class (which he subsequently painted gold). And what this Ray character just said about him will completely tick you off.

Your mouth will start to move before you can think. Before you wonder if you shouldn't just smile and say, "I don't know. Silly me," or something equally dumb. Instead, you'll take a step back and say, "Well, I guess I didn't think he was such a loser, or I wouldn't have dated him."

And then you'll leave that popular jerk standing alone on the dance floor.

It doesn't matter that you'll hide in the bathroom the rest of the night, wondering if you'd just committed social suicide (you hadn't).

Trust me when I tell you: This moment is one instance where that mouth of yours got it exactly right.

Even though it might have been easier, socially, to keep your mouth shut, you stood by a person that you really valued. You spoke the truth.

So try to be a little kinder when you're criticizing your sister's clothing, hair, and hygiene—but when it comes to standing up for the so-called losers of the world? Let your mouth do its thing.

Just—keep it away from Bill Underhill's tongue? A valiant mouth like yours doesn't need that kind of trauma.

P.S. Not getting along with Bill and Ray frees you up later to date an amazing boy... who kisses very well!

* All the names have been changed, because no one deserves to have his kissing technique trashed so publicly. Even if it was horrific.

Nikki

Nikki Loftin still talks too much and says inappropriate things in polite company. She and her Scottish husband are raising two sons who also mouth off—mostly to their parents. Nikki writes funny/scary stories for kids. Her debut novel, *The Sinister Sweetness of Splendid Academy*, came out in August 2012. Visit her at NikkiLoftin.com.

THE BEST DAYS OF OUR LIVES? REALLY?

Katherine Longshore

Dear Teen Me,

You know that they're lying to you.

You sit in a crowded auditorium, breathing the reek of stale French fries and dirty shoes. Assaulted by the clang and angst of a hundred other voices. And pitying the anonymous, faceless administrator calling for attention, announcing the title of the film you're about to see: *The Best Days of Your Life*.

Images of football games and track meets, homecoming queens and student government meetings crowd the screen, showering everyone with relentless cheer.

You stare into the screen onstage, with images of prom and chemistry flickering across it. And you imagine what's behind that screen: The worn boards, the black wing curtains, the jumble of leftover props from dozens of plays.

And that's what you want. Not the jerseys and pom-poms, but the props and rigging.

In your first role on that high school stage you'll play a catatonic mental patient. You'll sit in a heap for two hours. Not moving. Not speaking. Your only "line" will be a glass-shattering scream.

But then you'll go on to play an exiled Russian duchess, a head in a box (which eventually gets its cheerleader body back), a variety show MC, and a dead woman (the play is in flashback, and your part is actually the lead).

You'll nurture a deep love for theater—and it's not just because it gives you the chance to be the object of appreciation and applause. You'll fall in love with the character of Ariel at the Oregon Shakespeare Festival (and eventually you'll even have the chance to play the part in a circus tent in England). Sam Shepard will become your literary crush, and you'll never lose your desire to ride a streetcar as Blanche DuBois.

On that stage, you'll discover your place in this madhouse. Within this building—this architectural monstrosity that looks more like a prison than a place of education—you'll meet and bond and fall in love with people who will remain your friends throughout your entire life.

You may think they are lying to you at freshman orientation. Your memories won't include homecomings or basketball or dances filled with balloons and an endless loop of Duran Duran, Pat Benatar, and Huey Lewis. Nonetheless, your memories will root you to this place. To this moment. To this stage. To these people.

These days will not be the best of your life. (They can't rival the day you first set foot in Africa, or the day you married your best friend, or the moment when you first met your children, or got the call saying your novel was actually going to be published.) But they won't be the worst days either; they don't compare to the day you get battered on a deserted African road, or the day when you learn about your dad's cancer.

The truth is that your memories of these days will inspire you. They will perpetuate your love of literature—Ernest Hemingway, John Steinbeck, and Tennessee Williams. They'll remind you how to try your hardest, even when facing failure. They'll give you a taste for the unusual, and for diving into things just because they're new.

These days may not be the best days of your life, but like it or not, these days will define you. Live them.

Katherine Longshore

Katherine Longshore is the author of *Gilt* (2012), a novel of gossip and betrayal, queen bees, and treason, set in the court of King Henry VIII. Growing up, Katherine wanted to be an actress, but after a university semester abroad, she created her own major in cross-cultural studies and communications, planning to travel and write. Forever. Four years, six continents, and countless pairs of shoes later, she went to England for two weeks, stayed five years, and discovered history. She now lives in California with her husband, two children, and a sun-worshiping dog. Visit her at KatherineLongshore.com and at YAMuses.Blogspot.com.

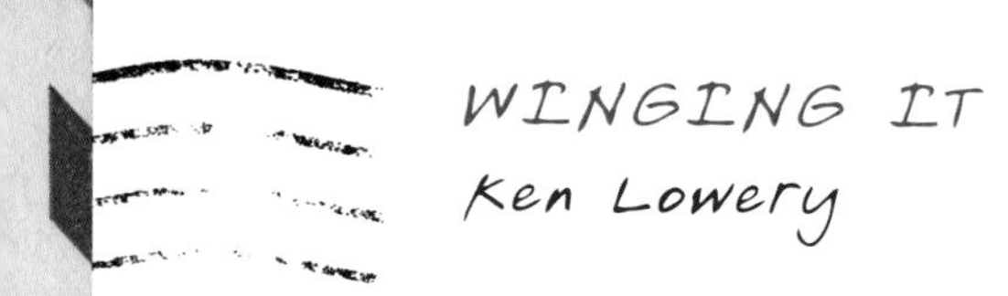

WINGING IT

Ken Lowery

Dear Teen Me,

It's me—that is, it's you, about thirteen years into the future. You have a great job that you love, you're happily married, and Bean is still the same cat that she was thirteen years ago. A black guy is president, and you voted for him. Craziest of all, you're internet famous—at least among a certain subset of professional word-fanciers and grammar pedants.

Now that I've blown your mind, let's get down to brass tacks: You're on your way to a major, depression-fueled meltdown. Some of that will be driven by simple, treatable biology; the rest, I'm sorry to say, has to do with some unhealthy notions you've got about what it means to be an adult.

The good news is that with a whole lot of therapy and some supernaturally wonderful friends and family, you will make it through to the other side. The bad news is that your unhealthy notions about adulthood still cast a shadow over everything you say and do.

Here's the source of your problems, in a nutshell: You believe that if you make it through high school, get into a good college (doesn't matter which one), and get your degree (likewise doesn't matter), you will then "grow up"—which to you means simply going through a kind of ceremony (after which—*presto*, you're mature), instead of actually evolving. Then, once you're among the ranks of the Mature Adults, you imagine that you'll know, more or less, exactly what to do for the rest of your time on earth.

This notion of life lived on autopilot seems like bliss to you, because it means an end to the struggle, an end to doubt. You will no longer cut classes or skip out on work for no reason. You will no longer stay up till 4:00 am and sleep in until 3:00 pm because you can't think of anything else to do. You will no longer respond to that beast of a question, "How are you feeling?" with your usual "I don't know," because your complete inability to articulate what goes on in your head will no longer matter.

This is a childlike vision of happiness, but it's also a vision of oblivion. In this vision, happiness means no longer having to think about, question, or make a decision about anything ever again.

Two things: One, outside of an airplane, there is no such thing as autopilot. All the other adults are making this shit up as they go along. They're *winging it.* The advice you've received from your elders and betters has helped you through a lot, but guess what: *They were winging it, too.* Adults and parents do not appear, fully formed, from Central Casting.

Two: The "winging it" stuff is okay. It's preferable, in fact, to the rosy-tinted nihilism you fantasize about now. Because being an adult means *knowing* that you're winging it, and being *okay* with that. Eventually, you'll realize this. Eventually, you'll see that "growing up" is an ongoing process, not a finish line. And you'll look back on what you've accomplished, what you've done, and what you've simply survived, and you'll trust yourself to move forward.

Life is full of uncertainty, yes, but *art* is born out of the same stuff. What you *can* and *will* be certain about, however, is that you can handle the uncertainty. That is a real strength

But credit where credit's due. You did get one thing right: All you have to do is hold on.

Ken Lowery is a co-creator and co-writer of the web television series *The Variants,* a co-creator of @FakeAPStylebook on Twitter, the editor of the @FakeAPStylebook spinoff book *Write More Good* (2011), the creator of @FakePewResearch, and just generally a dude who never met an idea he couldn't turn into a Twitter account. He is also a husband, which is surprising to him, and a copywriter in advertising, which is *very* surprising to him. Please do not give him more to do.

THE BALANCING ACT

Kekla Magoon

Dear Teen Me,

Put down that book and pay attention for a minute.

Someday soon, you'll live an amazing and very different kind of life than the one you're living now—but you'll have to put the books down and get out into the world before that can happen. I know how lonely you are. I know that what you want most is to have a best friend, someone that you can trust with your secrets and be real with, and who will hug you and tease you and accept you for who you really are. (Whatever that means.)

When you try to blend in it doesn't really work, does it? You're the only biracial girl in your class. That 'fro can't hide from nothin'. You don't feel black, so you don't fit in with the "real" black kids, but you don't look white, so you stand out among the white kids, too. But, when it comes down to it, you really don't need to try so hard to fit in. People actually like you. It's okay to be yourself and let down your guard.

It's not just being biracial that makes you feel different. Remember the time in gym class when that girl said you were probably a lesbian? Of course you remember. You thought about nothing else for weeks after, and it scared and confused you. Let it go. It scared you because it might have been a little bit true; it confused you because it wasn't totally true. You're going to love some guys in your life and you're going to love some girls, too, and that's fine. Most people aren't going to understand this about you, but you'll have to get used to that feeling, because it's never going to go away.

Everything about you is a little bit different. The way you look, the way you act, the way you *are*. You just have to remember to look at yourself in the mirror every morning and see yourself as beautiful. If you can manage to do that, the rest will take care of itself. It might be hard to believe that you will ever find your place in the world, but you will—once you start being truly yourself. Sometimes by just relaxing a little you can accomplish a lot.

There are going to be a lot of crazy ups and downs—once, for instance, in the course of a single week you'll go from crying on the floor of your apartment wondering where you'll get the money to pay your electric bill, to standing among a crowd of Hollywood celebrities, walking the red carpet. I kid you not.

Your whole life will be a balancing act, between having money and not having money, between being noticed and being ignored, between looking black and feeling white, between liking boys and liking girls. The key to finding your balance is feeling the earth beneath your feet and taking one step at a time. That will keep you grounded. Then, find the courage to stretch your arms a bit, and reach out for the things you want. Take some risks! Yes, this means showing your true colors, but it also means unfurling your wings. It's scary, but it will help. You won't ever feel surefooted, but you won't topple either.

This daily balancing act will turn you into your own kind of person: strong enough to stand alone, and unique, with a voice that rings out like morning thunder. And to think, they used to tease you for being so quiet. Your dreams are going to come true, and it's going to blow your mind.

Kekla Magoon

Kekla Magoon is the award-winning author of YA novels *The Rock and the River* (2009), *Camo Girl* (2011), *37 Things I Love* (2012), and *Fire in the Streets* (2012). She teaches writing to teens and adults, speaks at conferences, and visits schools and libraries to share her work. She lives in NYC… and at KeklaMagoon.com.

WHAT THE BULLY STOLE

Mari Mancusi

Dear Teen Me,

I've got an update for you from the future: Alex A. wrestles alligators for a living, and he loses every time.

Okay, okay, my update isn't completely nonfictional; I don't know that for sure. He might have ended up as a partner at a highly successful law firm. Or invented the inexplicably popular PajamaJeans (as seen on TV). For all I know he could've retired at twenty-nine after making a killing on his Apple stock. I don't know what he's actually doing these days, but I have to admit: I like to imagine his clothes reeking of swamp and defeat at the end of the workday.

I know, I know. It's not very nice to wish such misfortune on a former classmate. Especially one who might be off digging wells right now, so that thirsty children somewhere can have clean water to drink.

But I can't help it. I look back at the way he treated you in junior high and it still makes me furious.

Back then, not too many people talked about bullying. And even fewer did anything about it. If anything, parents had this crazy idea that whatever didn't kill you would make you stronger.

What total BS!

As if it wasn't hard enough for you to make the transition from a small private school to a huge public one. To leave your friends behind and get swallowed up in a sea of strangers. The only thing that made you feel at all safe was your art. The only place where no one could hurt you was a hand-drawn world of your own creation.

But did Alex A. understand this? Did he allow you to quietly escape your troubled reality for a rich hideaway of your own imagination? Nope. He crashed in, uninvited, invading your private world and publicly ridiculing you and your art. He exposed you and humiliated you in front of classmates you already had difficulty relating to. And when he had finished, you were so embarrassed you ripped up those once-precious drawings and threw them away in tears. You never picked up a pencil again.

You let Alex A. take something important from you. Something that mattered. Something that gave you comfort and hope. Today I can't draw to save my life. Alex stole that from me. From you. From us.

I don't know why Alex A. targeted you back then. Maybe he was feeling bad about himself and needed to rip into someone else to save his own self-esteem. Or maybe he sensed a sweet, sensitive soul who would take his cruelty to heart, giving him power for the first time in his life. But in the end, it doesn't matter why. He hurt you, and the experience didn't make you any stronger. It didn't make you a better person. Anyone who says bullying builds character can suck it.

But don't worry. In the end, you grow up to write a novel about bullying. You dig deep into your own psyche and fictionalize the pain you once experienced for real. And the best part? You give your heroine a happy ending. The kind you didn't get in real life. She rises above her haters. She doesn't let them rob her of her passion for art.

And the book winds up inspiring tons of teenage girls! Girls currently in junior high (and who are facing their own Alexes on a daily basis) take the time to write you e-mails telling you how your character's courage has helped them find some courage of their own.

So now that I think of it, maybe you did get your happy ending after all. While that little bully, Alex A., is busy trying to outwit (or outrun) a thousand-pound lizard.

Mari Mancusi

Emmy Award–winner **Mari Mancusi** works as a freelance TV producer and is the author of books for teens, including the Blood Coven Vampire series and *Gamer Girl* (2008). She lives in Austin, Texas, with her husband, Jacob, and their daughter, Avalon.

ALL THE WORLD'S A STAGE

Gretchen McNeil

Dear Teen Me,

You always needed the spotlight.

Not wanted. Not coveted. *Needed.*

Positive or negative, you needed the attention. You were the loudest kid at the party—the one most likely to accept a dare, or do something ridiculous to get a laugh. It's possible you hold the world record for the number of times you had to write "I will raise my hand before speaking" in the course of sixth grade. And the same thing goes for the number of trips to the principal's office (because you could never resist making that last witty comeback). Did you even consider how your mother would feel after the umpteenth time she was called in to discuss your behavior?

Your mom blames herself, but you both know it's not her fault. Your need for attention is so deeply rooted in your personality, so tangled up in your complicated emotional relationship with your absentee father, that there's no getting beyond it. At this point, you've spent so many years jumping through hoops to get him to notice you, that the behavior has become ingrained.

You got straight A's in school. Did that make him call? You were the star of the soccer team. Did that help him remember your birthday? You sang at graduation. Did that force him to show up? No, no, no.

I've got some bad news for you: He's never going to notice, acknowledge, remember, or even just show up. Never. But that doesn't stop you from trying.

But here's the good news: Extroverted attention-seekers have a perfect outlet on the stage.

Sure, you've been performing since you were a kid, but not in such a serious role, and never in a musical—with a curtain call all your own. Backstage, you're lined up, ready to take your solo bow in the spotlight. As you run out onstage, you're terrified, convinced that you're about to run into a mass of stares, and a few polite claps. But then it happens—and you'll remember that first curtain call for the rest of your life.

Is it just your imagination, or does the applause crescendo ever so slightly as you dip into a curtsy that would put Maria Callas to shame? You aren't the star of *Into the Woods*, but you had that audience in the palm of your hand. How? Why? Doesn't matter. Your heart is pounding in your chest, and you feel a powerful surge of adrenaline like you've never felt before.

You're hooked.

Later that night you'll remember that you invited your dad to come to opening night. You'd left messages on his home and work voicemails, messages that—as usual—would never be returned. It's the first time, perhaps, that you don't care. It's the beginning of the end—you won't jump through hoops for him anymore. The applause still echoes in your ears, the heat of the spotlight still burns on your cheeks. This flush of triumph is your new drug. From now on, you perform for yourself only.

The spotlight is yours.

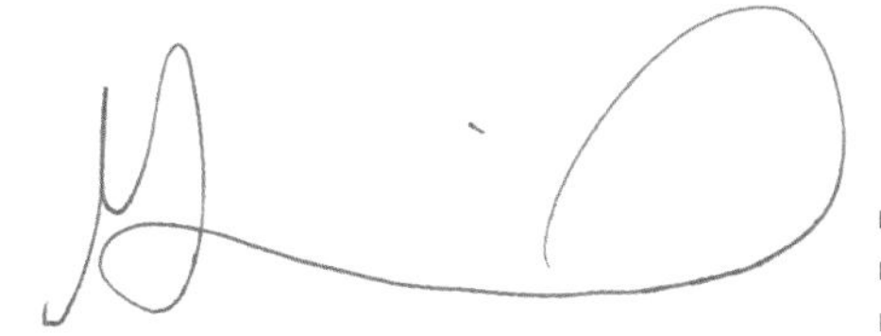

Gretchen McNeil is an opera singer, a writer, and a clown. Her young adult horror/paranormal novel *Possess* debuted in fall 2011. Her second novel, *Ten* (2012) is a young adult horror/suspense about ten teens trapped on a remote island with a serial killer. Gretchen is a former coloratura soprano, the voice of Mary on G4's *Code Monkeys*, and she currently sings with the L.A.-based circus troupe Cirque Berzerk. Gretchen is also a founding member of the vlog group the YARebels, where she can be seen as "Monday."

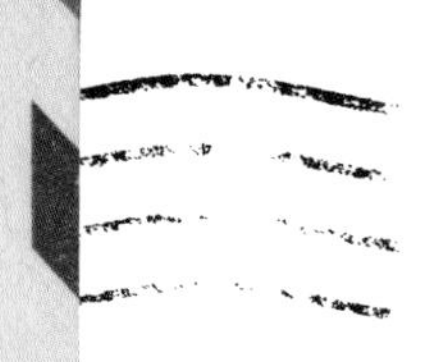

THE PURSUIT OF (MOMENTS OF) HAPPINESS

Jodi Meadows

Dear Teen Me,

I know how it is. Your parents are divorced, have been since you were four, and traveling between them is how you grew up. But now you're a teenager with school, work, and practice, and you don't have time to go back and forth. The days you used to visit Dad are now days you spend on your own, just doing your thing. Besides, Dad's changed a lot in the last few years. Visiting him isn't the same anymore.

Your dad is sick. You know it. You know about the alcoholism, the smoking, the diabetes, and the way he can get hurt by simply walking to the kitchen. You know he hasn't been *Dad* since he lost his job; he can't hold a new one, and his house is filthy. You know you don't enjoy visiting him anymore.

Here's what you're not recognizing: He's given up.

His kids aren't kids anymore. The adult kids have kids of their own. You and your sister visit Dad sometimes. You clean the house. You hassle him about drinking too much and remind him that smoking will give him lung cancer one day. You complain with your sister that it doesn't seem like he's even trying anymore.

He's not. He's killing himself, and he doesn't even care.

In a few years, you'll get married and move away. You'll try to talk to Dad on the phone, but you'll be lucky if he answers. And toward the end—though you won't realize it's the end—you won't be able to get hold of him at all. It's going to make you angry. You'll leave a lengthy voicemail about how he should answer the phone for his daughters if he wants to be involved in their lives.

You won't hear from him until he's found himself in the hospital, with cancer (yes, lung cancer) and a host of other problems. You won't even have time to fly back home to see him. Your sister is going to put him on the phone. He's going to sound heavily medicated (because he is), but you'll tell him you love him and that he has to get better. All the anger, all the bitterness—it won't matter anymore. You'll let it go, because he's your dad and you love him.

And that will be it. You'll be on the phone with your dad, and he'll be dying.

But you don't know about all that right now. Right now, you're frustrated. You know you'd rather just avoid the problem, and conveniently, that's not too hard to do at the moment. You've actually got a lot of other very legitimate things taking up your time, like work and school and practice.

But I wish you'd go to see him a little more often. Talk with him. Remind him that you love him. There's nothing you can do that will change the outcome. What happens to him is not your fault. It's a horrible collision of depression, addiction, and resignation. You can't change it, but you can give him a few more moments of happiness.

It may not seem like much right now, but in a few years you'll understand that those moments of happiness can really make a difference.

Jodi Meadows

Jodi Meadows lives and writes in the Shenandoah Valley with her husband, a cat, and an alarming number of ferrets. She is a confessed book addict who has wanted to be a writer ever since she decided against becoming an astronaut. She is the author of *Incarnate* (2012) and *Asunder* (2013). Visit her at JodiMeadows.com.

THIS IS NOT YOUR STORY

Saundra Mitchell

Dear Teen Me,

All right, look. You didn't kill him.

You're going to spend tonight in the laundry room, sitting on the dryer. Shuttered doors closed, and phone pulled as far as the cord will go, so you can complain about it to your best friend.

Your idiot brother, who swallows all the energy in the family, who screws up everything, is at the hospital. Again. Last time, he was drunk and passed out and nearly burned his foot off at his makeshift camp in the woods.

And today, you came home from school and he was drunk. Again. You could tell because of all the empty beer cans in the living room. He was passed out, again. You could tell by the way he was sprawled across the living room carpet. With his stupid mouth agape. With his stupid hand on his stupid chest.

Was he going to wake up? You dug your toes into his ribs, way harder than you had to, and pushed. Pushed hard. Later, you'll think you kicked him, like straight-up soccer-goal kicked him, but you didn't. Guilt magnifies things, but the truth is, you shoved him, and he didn't wake up.

So you called mom and bitched, "He's drunk. Again."

You called your best friend and bitched, "He's drunk. Again."

But there's a family history with alcohol. You've got a bunch of extended relatives who all have an extended relationship to the hooch (it's funny how we're all kind of proud of the grandmother who bootlegged during Prohibition). You know that passed out drunks usually wake up. Or move. Or something.

So when you got nervous, and checked to see if he was breathing, he *was*. His heart was beating. And he *did* smell like beer. You *did* call your mother. That's it. Those are the facts in evidence. As soon as you realized that all the pill bottles in the kitchen window were empty, you did the right thing.

You called Mom. You called Dad. You helped them carry your brother to the car in a green and yellow crocheted blanket so they could take him to the hospital. You knew better than to call 911, because ambulances are expensive, and nobody in the family can afford them.

And now you're holed up in the laundry room, air thick and warm and spring fresh, and you're going to rail about it for a while. How he always does this. How he runs away on the holidays and screws up birthdays, and how he's so busy destroying everything around him that you may as well not even exist.

After a while, you'll get scared. You'll bluster about how you're going to kill him when he gets home from the hospital. Eventually, you'll just hope. When the other line rings, you won't say anything when your mother tells you that your brother is dead.

You won't hear anything, either. Later, the details will get filled in, passively, randomly. Pumped his stomach, but it was already too late. Took all of his antidepressants, blood alcohol level was negligible.

You'll go through his room and discover somebody else was in the house that day, because all of his Metallica tapes are missing. There will be a funeral where you walk out on God, and so many people in the house, and for some reason, Mom will bring that yellow and green blanket home.

When you get evicted from public housing—bloodlessly informed that you no longer meet minimum occupation requirements for a three-bedroom apartment—the blanket will go with you. In the new apartment, it'll be there, on the couch. On the chair. You'll put it away and wish you could burn it. It's a shroud, exactly the shape of death; you'll hate it because sometimes you'll need a break from hating yourself.

But that afghan didn't kill him, and neither did you. It doesn't matter that you tried to OD two years ago, taking pills off that same windowsill. He wasn't thinking about *you* that day. It wasn't *your* idea. You didn't pull the trigger; there wasn't even a trigger to be pulled. Your brother was mentally ill and couldn't get the treatment he needed. He self-medicated until he couldn't self-medicate any more. It had nothing to do with you.

Nevertheless, it's going to be a while (a couple of decades at least) before you realize all that. Before you realize that we're *all* dead for longer than we're ever alive. Before you realize that shoving him with your foot isn't the same as kicking him with jackboots. Before you understand that you were there that day, you were one of the players, but the story wasn't about you at all.

Once upon a time, there was a sick little boy, and he killed himself six months before his fifteenth birthday. He had a sister, and she cannot forget.

But know that eventually, you can forgive. Him. Yourself. The world. You'll write a book and put his name on the dedication page. That's the best you'll be able to do, a little bit of immortality catalogued by the Library of Congress.

And today, you did the best that you could. Start the dryer again, because the sound is soothing, and wait for the call that's coming. It changes everything, but listen to me; this is the truth:

You didn't kill him. It's not your fault.

Saundra Mitchell has been a phone psychic, a car salesperson, a denture deliverer, and a layout waxer. She's dodged trains, endured basic training, and hitchhiked from Montana to California. She teaches herself languages, raises children, and makes paper for fun. She's also the author of *Shadowed Summer* (2009), *The Vespertine* (2011), *The Springsweet* (2012), and the forthcoming *Mistwalker*. She always picks truth; dares are too easy.

Q and A:

WHAT WAS YOUR FIRST JOB?

"Dog walking, I was thirteen. I lived in NYC so there was a pick-up-poop law. That part was kinda nasty, but I was so proud to be earning my own money. Spent most of it on candy, which we didn't have in the house."

Tracy White

~

"Movie theater popcorn popper."

Cynthia Leitich Smith

~

"McDonalds, represent! I was 15 and worked the front register. Try not to be too jealous."

Rhonda Stapleton

~

"Teaching piano at Lecuona Academy."

Caridad Ferrer

~

"I worked for my best friend's family at the carnival. They ran concession stands and I made funnel cake, sold cotton candy and caramel apples, and scooped sno-cones. That syrup does not come off."

Jessica Corra

~

"Cutting wood and selling it by the side of the road."

Kersten Hamilton

~

"I was a teenage tax collector. Seriously! By the time I was fourteen, I could talk knowledgeably about "millage" and the fiscal benefits of waiting until the "face period" to pay your real estate taxes."

Beth Fantaskey

"Fry cook at White Castle."

Marke Bieschke

"Paperboy!"

Geoff Herbach

"Writer."

Riley Carney

"Vacuuming the floors at Barbara Ann's, a department store 'down the back' in Secaucus. Practically every girl in town worked there as a salesgirl, and I vacuumed. Needless to say, I gossiped more than I worked!"

Michael Griffo

"Washing greasy dishes at a roadside diner."

Katherine Longshore

"I started my own babysitting service when I was twelve. A quarter an hour."

Ilsa J. Bick

"Babysitter, then lifeguard."

Lauren Oliver

"I was a canvasser for the League of Conservation Voters when I was 14. I got mugged on my third day. Nobody believed me."

Carrie Jones

~

"Mucking stalls in my aunt's barn. (FYI, mucking stalls means shoveling out the horse poop.)"

Tera Lynn Childs

~

"Working at the local McDonald's. I was even in a national commercial for them."

Heather Davis

~

"Babysitting a nine-year-old demon spawn all summer when I was 13. First 'real' job, where I got the minimum wage? I was a hostess at the K Bob's Steakhouse."

Nikki Loftin

~

"Babysitter, followed by camp counselor, followed by one of those people who dresses up in colonial costume and gives tours of The Freedom Trail."

Leila Sales

~

"Waiting tables at Paco's Mexican Grill when I was fifteen. I came home smelling like chips and salsa everyday. It was pretty gross."

Stacey Jay

~

"McDonald's cashier, complete with polyester uniform that gave me a rash in my armpits."

Amy Kathleen Ryan

~

GET BETTER
Hannah Moskowitz

Dear Teen Me,

So you have this CD you burned a few weeks ago, and you've listened to it God knows how many times now, because ever since you got your license you've hardly left your car. It's just easier to drive around and go out for coffee (which you don't like) with boys (who you don't like) than it is to go home and stare at all the food you want to eat and cry over the 94 percent on your test (because *what about the other six points*). Because then you eventually just have to go to bed for your four hours of sleep before you have to repeat the whole thing again...and again...and again.

Lately you have an extra hour in the car every week, because you're driving to and from therapy trying to shake that eating disorder.

You're about to turn seventeen, and it doesn't matter how much you want to get out of the house and listen to those same songs again and again and again; driving scares the crap out of you (it still does), so half the time you call and cancel the therapy appointments five minutes before they're due to start, which means your parents still get charged the full amount, which means your parents probably think you're going, but instead you lie on the floor and count your ribs, and you've never hated yourself as much as you do when you see what you are doing to your mother all the hell over her face. You take pictures of yourself sucking in your stomach and leave them on her camera because you just don't care anymore, because this stopped being fun a long time ago, and your favorite clothes are too big, and now the only good part of any of this is that CD.

I'm listening to the songs I can remember from it while I write this, and I'm right back there in the parking lot where you used to park illegally, sitting in the car instead of going in to therapy, seat pushed all the way back, crying so hard you can't breathe. I'm there too. Pretend I'm there the whole time, okay?

Because I haven't forgotten. I remember you, Hannah.

And I know what you want to hear more than anything else in the world, what you're dying to hear, what you want so much to be true—and *listen to me,* because it *is* true. Ready?

This isn't normal.

It's *not.* It's not normal and you don't have to go through it. You're not weak. You're a chick with some messed up brain chemistry, and you're crying in the parking lot afraid to take meds because you think you won't be able to write anymore if things don't hurt this much.

About six months ago you wrote that book about the kid who wants to break all his bones (and in about a year and a half people are going to start asking you, "How do you know so much about self-injury?" and you're going to smile and talk around the question). A few days from now, you're going to be standing on the sidewalk outside your therapist's office when your agent calls and tells you that you're going on submission, but she's going to tell the publishers you're seventeen, okay, because no one wants to work with a sixteen-year-old, and *God*, can you understand, because you have to *live* with a sixteen-year-old and you have to watch your parents try to live with a sixteen-year-old and you'd get out of all of that somehow if you knew how. (You don't get out. You stay. And thank you for that, Hannah. Thank you for that every single day.)

Your therapist asks questions you don't know how to answer. You think maybe turning seventeen will help, and then you turn seventeen and it gets worse and junior year slips through your fingers. You sleep through prom and your best friend's graduation. You get your lowest GPA ever. It's unacceptable, because if you don't get into Brown, you don't know what you'll do.

(You get into Brown. After the first month, you're ready to get the hell out of there. You transfer home to the huge state school you refused to ever apply to. It's incredible.)

Look.

It's not normal.

You're not normal.

And I know that if I were there really sitting in the car next to you, and you heard these words—words that everyone else in the world would probably think are horrible—you would latch onto them. Because *yes*, I understand. You are not overreacting and you are not imagining that things really are unfathomably difficult, and you are so not alone.

It really should not be this hard to get out of bed. You really should not be *that* angry *all* the time. It's not hormones and it's not a phase, and *I believe you*, and you should have actually talked to that therapist and reached out and gotten the help you needed a long time ago, because you're going to keep doing this for *years*, and it just does not have to be this hard.

"Suffering for your art" is just a pretty phrase people say, okay?

But you're not going to listen, and you're going to keep doing this to yourself for a long time.

You'll probably be surprised at what fixes itself when you get better. Things that seem irreparably broken now, like your relationship with your mom? You two are going to have an amazing relationship. Your best friend who's doing even worse than you are? She's okay now, too.

Those songs you listened to while you drove to therapy and out for coffee with boys or around your neighborhood and thought about food the entire way every time? Those songs are eating disorder songs and will be until the day you die. You broke those songs.

But it's okay. Because here I am, as better as it really gets, listening to those songs and remembering you.

What's funny is that I can't write a good story that's in any way related to your eating disorder. I've tried, believe me, because everyone's always telling me to write what I know, but the truth is, your ED ruined that story for me, because now it's full of details that aren't important and don't make any larger sense, and they're clogging up the big picture and I'm so filled with shame when I try to type that I can't ever make it sound real. You took that story off the table. It's the same reason that when you wanted to write a book with self-injury, you had to have the kid break his bones, because you took all the normal stuff off the table, didn't you? You stole the stories. You keep stealing stories.

Stop. Leave me something to work with. Don't make me try to make art out of your suffering. It doesn't work.

Get better.

Get better.

Get better.

And get a fucking move on, because I have all these books to write and you need to not use up any more stories because I'm bad enough at coming up with ideas as it is, okay?

Go make up new stories and live things that are too beautiful and unreal and stupid and happy to make their way into books.

I'll be here.

Hannah Moskowitz is the author of multiple books for teens, including *Break* (2009), a YALSA Popular Paperback for Teens, *Invincible Summer* (2011), and *Gone, Gone, Gone* (2012), as well as several books for younger readers. She is a student at the University of Maryland and she wouldn't be a teenager again if you paid her. This whole author thing is all just an excuse for her to get to talk to people, so visit her at HannahMosk.Blogspot.com and say hi, okay?

WHAT I REALLY WANT

Jenny Moss

Dear Teen Me,

It's your senior year.

You're in English class, at a desk in the back corner of the room, with a point to make about Hester Prynne in *The Scarlet Letter*, but your teacher turns away, her wiry black and silver hair shaking, as she laughs with the cheerleaders and student council members, and you want...What?...What is it you want?

I see your confusion. You're so distracted by those around you that you don't know what you want.

So listen to me for a moment.

Think of your wildest dreams.

Talking with Hemingway and Fitzgerald about art, life, and things that matter *until late into the night at a smoky Parisian bistro...*

Catching a glimpse of a nervous Shakespeare gathering his actors before they take the stage in the court of Elizabeth I...

Laughing at Dorothy Parker's quips at the Algonquin...

Those might not be possible. Try again.

Studying literature at a centuries-old university...

Writing in longhand at a French café...

Watching the Tuscan countryside roll by, with your backpack at your side and your journal in your lap...

Grab hold of those dreams.

Put aside your need to do the practical thing. Research far-flung colleges. Find a guidance counselor. Dream more, dream bigger, dream wilder.

Ask: "What do *I* want? *What* do I want? What do I *want?*"

Read. (Wait—you already do that.) Read more. Keep reading.

Seek advice. Think. Listen.

Understand that what works for someone else might not work for you. (Example: those red Coca-Cola pants and top your mother thought would look great on you.)

Understand that not everyone sees the world as you do. (Example: Not everyone hears beauty and mystery and magic when Bob Dylan sings.)

Understand that there are other paths. (Example: Studying physics at a college an hour from your house is just one choice.)

Be patient, but act. Sometimes the worst decision is no decision.

Make mistakes. Change your mind. It'll be okay.

Remember: Your greatest strength is your greatest weakness is your greatest strength. Things will make more sense if you can come to terms with that.

Your dreams? Remember those? Are you still holding on?

So...ignore that English teacher who loves only the popular kids. You have a future she won't be a part of. Ignore those girls who are laughing at you now. You have more important things to think about. Instead, listen to the voice inside of you, the one saying, *I want to be part of the conversation*.

Keep writing in private. You're getting better.

Keep doing math. You love it.

Keep singing in the church choir. You may be tone-deaf, but God hears you perfectly.

Consider the following: You *can* be in a Montparnasse café or at the Algonquin Hotel on a 1920s evening, and you can talk to anyone you want about anything you want....

If that's what you really want, find a way.

Jenny Moss is an author of historical fiction and fantasy. Her titles include *Winnie's War* (2009), *Shadow* (2010), and *Taking Off* (2011). As a teen, she dreamed of moving to Europe and writing in small cafés. Instead, she became an engineer and trained astronauts. She now lives in Austin, Texas, and makes up stories for a living.

DANCING WITH THE DEAD

Sarah Ockler

Dear Teen Me,

Prom is the most important night of your life.

That's what everyone keeps telling you, anyway. A night to remember, they say. Something you'll reflect on with fondness and joy and maybe a bit of longing, too, when you can no longer stuff that thirty-something ass into your teen-something poofy-sleeved dream dress.

Hey, you only live once, right?

Screw that.

Thing is, you don't have a boyfriend. And yeah, you could invite one of your guy friends from another school, or go stag. But...*stag*. Do you really want to spend another weekend bobbing around the dance floor in an awkward, gyrating clump with your few remaining girlfriends, arms entwined, belting out those heartbreaking Bon Jovi ballads? You're practically a college woman, for the love of hair spray. Who needs prom?

Um...pretty much everyone you know, apparently.

And though you don't solicit their to-go-or-not-to-go advice, your classmates are happy to dish it out. You'll regret it, they warn! You'll miss out on the most magical, momentous night of your life!

Honestly, you feel kinda sad that some people believe the most magical, momentous night of their entire lives could *possibly* be over and done with before their eighteenth birthday. I mean, you haven't even experienced a proper orgasm yet, let alone Indian food or marrying your best friend or a road trip to the Grand Canyon or climbing the highest mountain in Colorado or writing a book (all coming in due time). But this won't stop the rite of passage do-gooders from trying to convince you otherwise, what with their vivid depictions of your promless future and all. Stopping them would take an act of God. Or maybe...

The Grateful Dead.

The Dead are coming to town on prom weekend, you gleefully discover! Soon the entire county will be overrun by patchouli-scented, pot-smokin', peace-lovin'

Deadheads, and if magical moments are what you're after, you can't think of a better crowd to inspire a few.

The decision is easy now. You're ditching prom to hang out with the Dead. And your best friend, Melissa, is coming with you. Neither of you has enough cash to buy tickets, but that's okay. You'll show up anyway, hang out on the grounds, and catch a few riffs from the open-air arena.

When the big night arrives, you pack Melissa's old Civic with blankets and snacks and all your raging, naked excitement and head to the stadium, high on rebellion and big-eyed dreams. The grounds are alive with cars and buses, tents, girls in long skirts, and boys kicking hacky sacks and blowing bubbles into the sky. Campfires and hot dogs and earthy sage spice the air, and you close your eyes and take it all in, memorizing every detail.

Melissa pulls the gold Civic into a disorganized tangle of cars that stretches into the next county. There's a faded red and white NO PARKING sign, but you come to the only logical conclusion: It's a concert. They can't *possibly* tow everyone.

You leave the car beneath the sign and meld into the crush of barefooted, hairy-legged Deadheads meandering toward the stadium. People sell beer out of giant ice chests; others sell weed out of Whitman's Sampler boxes. You pass by these industrious, homegrown vendors until a better offer catches your attention.

"Free hugs," a twenty-something guy calls out. He's cute; seems like a fair deal. You take him up on the offer. He's a good hugger, too, and you get your money's worth. Perfect, since you've only got fifteen bucks to your name.

You find a good spot on the grass outside the stadium and stretch out on a blanket the color of the sky. You and Melissa watch the sunset, sipping two sugary wine coolers that her brother snagged for you. Music floats on the air, drifting on pale purple smoke into the night. All around you, baby Deadheads toddle naked through the grass while women braid their hair and men sway in trippy, rhythmic circles. You fantasize about them. About dropping out and falling in with a new family, traveling the country, following the music. You're a writer, after all, and there's a story in that kind of life. You're a hippie, too, deep down where it counts. You want to grow vegetables and braid your hair and walk around smelling like the earth. You want to learn the words to all the songs, to understand the stuff that Jerry Garcia sings about.

To unravel the mystery of why good music always makes you cry.

But that's for the future, maybe. Tonight, you're just happy to be there.

Sometime after the first set, the stadium doors open, and security calls you forth, ushering in the poor, ticketless masses for a chance to see the stage. The Dead, it turns out, welcome all. You're entranced. When you reach the top of the stairs and step out into the stands, your heart flutters. Jerry's leading the band in this *crazy* jam, part jazz riff, part folksy drum trip. There are no words, just rich music, and everyone in the packed stadium sways and spins, hands floating up like little birds. Colored lights illuminate the stage, and though you're way up high, the energy reaches you and fills you with an inexplicable human connectedness the likes of which you'll never again feel. Soon, your hands float up like the rest, and you dance.

At the end of the show, you drift on the current of the crowd, flowing outside like water. You don't speak, but you look at your best friend and smile, eyes shining. It's that kind of night, and you drop your last fifteen bucks on a T-shirt to commemorate it. "Toke up, Doc," it says under a red-eyed Bugs Bunny doing just that.

(FYI, the shirt isn't *exactly* a crowd-pleaser with school officials that Monday, or with your parents, but that's a story for another letter.)

You and Melissa are so enraptured that you don't immediately notice the cop looking out across the field, standing in the empty spot where Melissa's car ought to be. The illegally parked vehicles have been impounded, he announces. You can reclaim them at the station for a fee of one hundred and eighty-five dollars.

You look at the shirt in your hands.

That's all, folks.

You're stranded.

You could take your chances at Camp Deadhead, you think. Put that fantasy in motion, find a nice dreadlocked family and share their wool blankets until it's time to shove off at dawn....

No. Look around. Take a deep breath of tea-scented air and assess the situation. There's trash everywhere, cans and bottles overflowing from barrels, dotting the grass like aluminum flowers.

Five-cent-deposit-earning aluminum flowers.

Free Hugs Guy, still standing where you'd left him earlier in all his dreadlocked, tie-dyed, hugs-for-all glory, overhears your predicament and offers to help. He doesn't have any money, either, since he didn't make a profit that night, but he's not as reluctant to approach random strangers for help. He's also fluent in Stoner. With his guidance, you scrounge up a quarter for the pay phone and call Melissa's mom, who's accustomed to your stranger-than-fiction antics and who, critical to the plan taking shape in your mind, owns a minivan.

I'm not gonna lie. Free Hugs Guy and his utter selflessness are long gone by the time the minivan rolls up. It's three hours of backbreaking labor to collect enough glass and metal, using your sky-blue blanket as a net and heaving it, one trip at a time, into the cavernous minivan. By the time you cash in at the grocery store, you're bleary-eyed and delirious, but you earn nearly two hundred bucks—four thousand cans' and bottles' worth.

Enough to free the car and snag a box of doughnuts for the ride home, way too many hours past curfew.

That show was one for the archives.

You witnessed history that night. Two years later, Jerry Garcia will be dead. The prom show will end up being the band's last appearance in town.

And you were there.

In some ways, your classmates are right. You *will* look back on prom night with fondness and joy. And for the rest of your life, people will swear that prom *was* the most magical, momentous night of their lives, and they'll wonder, as they did then, whether you regret ditching the dance. But I promise you something: You'll *never* regret it. Not once.

Because you got to dance with the Dead.

And twenty years later, in the quiet that follows your most magical, momentous nights, sometimes you'll catch yourself singing an old song with your eyes closed, and you'll remember those crazy riffs and the sky-blue blanket full of bottles and you'll smile, your heart full and content.

Sarah Ockler is the best-selling author of *Fixing Delilah* (2010) and the critically acclaimed *Twenty Boy Summer* (2009), a YALSA Teens' Top Ten nominee and IndieNext pick. When she's not writing or reading at home in Colorado, Sarah enjoys taking pictures, eating cupcakes, hugging trees, and road-tripping through the country with her husband, Alex. Check out her latest young adult novel, *Bittersweet* (2012), and visit her at SarahOckler.com.

BEST FRIENDS FOREVER (FOR REAL)

Lauren Oliver and Elizabeth Miles

Dear Teen Elizabeth (from Lauren Oliver),

First off, let me say: You really got me through high school. Without your support and friendship, I'm not sure I would have made it out. So, thank you. I'm very happy to tell you that you will grow into a beautiful, accomplished, and beloved young woman, and I'm even happier to tell you that you and I will remain best friends.

There are a few other pieces of information I'd like to send along your way, so bear with me.

✶ 1. First off, your hair looks super cute when it's really short. Go ahead and lop it off! You'll look like a beneficent pixie.

✶ 2. Secondly, DON'T SMOKE. Seriously. Put down the cigarettes NOW. If you don't, you and I will struggle with quitting throughout our twenties. It totally isn't worth it.

✶ 3. Remember all those boys who broke our hearts over the years? There was Brett (you), Dan Waitman (me), Steve (me again), Brett again (you); there were Jons and Adams and Matts and countless others. Sometimes we suffered for days or weeks. Sometimes we cried, sometimes we starved, and sometimes we couldn't stop eating—but we always leaned on each other (and on an occasional dose of *Pride and Prejudice* and a certain Mr. Colin Firth) to get us through.

I won't say now that those experiences weren't worth it, but you should know that they were just like the math problems we had to do in calc—their greatest worth was that they taught us *process*. In the case of calc, we learned how to think; in the case of the Toms, Jons, and Adams, we learned how to how to feel and to love. It wasn't about the particulars, but the generals: All that heartbreak helped us learn how to heal, and it helped us become better and better at relationships.

✶ 4. Your parents are great in some ways and crazy in others. So are mine. They won't necessarily understand us any better as we get older. But we can understand them better, and understand that they have their own

issues and limitations that are absolutely *not* reflections of us. Your parents love you and they're doing the best they can.

- 5. Don't be afraid to ask for help when you need it. You're going to go through some dark times. I'll be there for you. So will Laura and Jackie. So will Dafna, who will become your best friend in college, and so will various other people who love you. Lean on us.
- 6. Go to therapy!
- 7. You're going to be tempted to move to DC and go to grad school some day. Skip that whole section of your life; go straight to Portland, Maine. You'll love it there.
- 8. You may not know this, but I was really jealous of you in high school. Boys always seemed to fall in love with you, and rightly so. And I felt they always just used me because of my somewhat...*questionable* morals and attitudes. Anyway, I just want to say: That was my problem, not yours, and I'm sorry. You deserve to be loved. So do I, for that matter!
- 9. Don't let me get so drunk at your house in Otis after prom!! Ugh. I thought I was going to die.
- 10. You'll be okay. You'll be more than okay. You'll be great.

Love,

Dear Teen Lauren (from Elizabeth Miles),

I can't believe we ever hated each other. Remember that? How you thought I was always either laughing hysterically or sobbing (true), and how I thought you were a snob (also true)? Thank God for Alanis Morissette and eggs with ketchup and *Pride and Prejudice* and the Beatles and the rest of the random and wonderful things we eventually bonded over. If not for them, I may have missed out on a truly rewarding friendship with an impressive, generous, beautiful woman. I've read your letter, and in response—and in order to thank you for being my best friend, then and now—I've compiled some of my own advice tidbits:

- 1. My hair looks good short? Yours looks good—striking, really—when it's combed.
- 2. DON'T SMOKE! It's the worst. It's an expensive habit that will give us wrinkles! Who wants wrinkles?!
- 3. You are one sexy *chica* and you can *work* it. You know it, I know it, boys know it, and girls know it. It's a complicated thing, being a woman who is both seductive and smart—and that balancing act doesn't get any easier as you get older. Rest assured, your charms go far beyond your pretty face, hot body, and racy sense of adventure. Don't exploit yourself. Trust in the fact that you're loved now, and that you'll continue to be loved in the future, for much more than your sex appeal.
- 4. We had a list in the back of our shared journal: "Hook-Up Deal-Breakers and Makers." That list may not be as relevant these days (not least because of that ring on your finger), but its underlying philosophy is right on: *We deserve the best*. It's okay to say what we want and to identify what we don't.
- 5. You're going to experience some terrible losses—too much, too early. Do what you can in these teenage years to make yourself resilient, to understand that bad things happen to good people, to cultivate sources of support both internal and external that you can rely on when your worst-case scenarios become reality.
- 6. Totally, go to therapy.
- 7. Even though we were best friends, we never really talked about "popularity" per se. That's probably a good thing—we were too busy trying to remember our harmonies for Quaker Notes. But despite having a sizeable group of friends and being involved in several inclusive school activities, I know I was still *worried that so-and-so doesn't like me*, and *secretly thrilled to have been invited to that party*, etc. First of all, teenage Lauren, let's be open with each other about these concerns. And second of all, if you have them too, just know that we'll realize SOON after high school which friendships matter and which ones don't—in fact, the closeness that you, I, Laura, and Jackie share is an anomaly, not the norm. Now, eleven years after high school, I talk to precisely four people who I knew back then.
- 8. Just like I should skip my hemp-necklace-wearing phase, you should pass over the faux-bling-wearing phase (wait until you can afford the real stuff)—hippie chic and gaudy baubles don't really suit us.

- 9. Maybe pressure me to hand in at least *one* of my AP European History assignments on time? How do you *do* it? ("It," in this case, means having a relatively normal teenage life *and* getting straight A's—God, I was *so* envious!)
- 10. You may not know it now, but babes, you're gonna blow everyone away.

Love,

Eliz Miles

Lauren Oliver is the *New York Times* best-selling author of *Before I Fall* (2011) and the Delirium trilogy. She is also the author of *Liesl and Po* (2011), a book for younger readers, which received two starred reviews. Kirkus had this to say about it: "With nods to Dahl, Dickens, the Grimms and even Burnett, the author has made something truly original." Lauren thinks you'll like it too! She is also a cofounder of the literary development company Paper Lantern Lit (PaperLanternLit.com). Find out more at LaurenOliverBooks.com.

Elizabeth Miles is the debut author of *Fury* (2011), the first book in the Fury series. *Fury* is a paranormal thriller that's been compared to Stephen King, '80s horror movies, and *Gossip Girl.* (Elizabeth can't decide which of those comparisons she likes best.) A journalist by day, Elizabeth lives in Portland, Maine, with her boyfriend and two cats. She and Lauren have been besties since eighth grade. Learn more at ElizabethMilesBooks.com or TheFurySeries.com.

JUST BE YOURSELF!

Stephanie Pellegrin

Dear Teen Me,

Psst! Hey! You in the corner of the library with your nose stuck in a book. Yes, you. Don't recognize me without that awful perm, do you? (Remind me again why you thought that was a good idea?)

Anyway, I hope you don't mind if I sit with you for a minute, but we need to talk. Don't worry about the "no talking in the library" rule. I'm sure we'll be fine. Librarians aren't as bad as they seem.

Judging from the hair and braces I'd have to guess you're in your junior year. Yes? Thought so. I'd forgotten how many lonely lunch hours you spent in the school library. You have some friends in the cafeteria that you could sit with, but you don't feel like you really fit in, do you? That's why you joined every school club you could. I just counted and you're in eighteen, not to mention the numerous after-school activities you're involved in. I mean honestly, you joined the ROTC. You don't even *like* ROTC! And I won't even bother bringing up that time you tried ballet. I'm still having nightmares about the fifth position!

Let me ask you, how's it all working out? Not very well, am I right? By spending so much time trying to *find* yourself, you're slowly *losing* yourself. We don't all have one single rock-star talent, and honestly, I think those of us who don't are the lucky ones. Life isn't about finding the one thing you're good at and never doing anything else; it's about exploring yourself and finding out who you really are on your own terms and in your own way. You don't have to exhaust yourself to do that.

Oh, don't be so down in the dumps about it. You'll eventually find something you're good at, I promise. It's a long, winding road to get there, but you'll find it. Being able to spend all day doing what you love (or one of the things that you love) is the most amazing feeling in the world. And no, I won't tell you what it is, so don't even ask me. Just remember to always be yourself, because there's nobody else who can do it for you. I think E. E. Cummings put it best when he said, "It takes courage to grow up and become who you really are."

Looks like the bell is about to ring so I'll leave you to your book. What are you reading, anyway? Oh, *The Last Battle* by C. S. Lewis. I should have guessed. You should give those Harry Potter books a try. I saw you roll your eyes! I know they seem like just another fad, but trust me, they're better than you think. They've got a real future!

Stephanie Pellegrin

Stephanie Pellegrin wrote her first novel in second grade. It was about a boy heart who falls in love with a girl heart only to find out her "heart" belongs to another. She now writes young adult and middle-grade fiction. She is involved in the Austin, Texas, chapter of Society of Children's Book Writers and Illustrators, and is a cofounder of Literary Lonestars, a Facebook group dedicated to Texas bloggers and authors. Stephanie currently lives with her husband in Austin.

FIRST KISS

Mitali Perkins

Dear Teen Me,

I know you've liked him—adored him, really—for full-on two years now. But somehow, nobody knows about it, not even friends who share their crushes in intimate detail. You pour the truth only into journals stashed deep in desk drawers.

He's a basketball star with strawberry-blonde hair and blue eyes. You? The only dark-skinned girl in school—a straight-A nerd, trying to obey traditional Hindu parents and squandering babysitting money on trendy jeans.

But you both play tennis. And he needs help in English class. So you're friends.

Now it's junior year. You're losing hope. You think there's no way he's going to like you. Not in that way, not a chance. When you're standing in a group of white girls, the guys look right past you.

But wait. Be patient. Let me show you something....

"Want to go to the amusement park with a bunch of us this Saturday?" he asks, passing your table on the way to eat lunch with his basketball buddies.

You're with your regulars, but he's looking at you. Right at you. Only at you.

"Sure," you say, managing to keep your voice as easy and relaxed as his.

The regulars are quiet, but only for a bit. You see them shrug and shake it off. A blip, for sure. Guys ask *them* out in front of you, not vice versa, right? You're the confidante they trust around that boyfriend with a wandering eye: You're not quite invisible but you are safely neutered. Loveless but beloved.

Saturday dawns, a breezy, summery Santa Cruz–perfect day. You chat with the others on the drive, but once you get into the park and ride the carousel twice, everybody else disappears.

I promise this will happen. Don't give up.

Your head buzzes with the nearness of him as you twist and turn on the roller coaster. You almost taste the sweetness of his smile as he wins a stuffed bear and hands it to you. But you've become an expert at hiding your passion. The buddy banter continues and you avoid his eyes.

On the ride home, tired and squashed in the back with the others, you won't talk. But he rests an arm along the back of the seat, his T-shirt soft against your neck. Your ponytail brushes his skin. Will he feel how fast your heart is beating? You pretend to watch the scenery. He closes his eyes after the sunset.

One by one, the others get dropped off. Now it's just the two of you in the backseat, but he won't slide to the other window. No, he stays close, denim leg against yours, his free-throwing arm still stretched out behind you. You make yourself not lean into him in the darkness.

As the car stops in front of your house, his eyes flick to the rearview mirror. You open the door and swing a leg out. "Thanks so much," you say.

In one quick move, as smooth and agile as when he scores a layup at the buzzer, he leans over and kisses your cheek. "You're beautiful," he whispers.

The car pulls away.

You won't remember how long you stand outside the house.

You'll forget if the night was starry or if the plums on the tree were ripe.

But you'll never forget that kiss, soft on your cheek. Those words, spoken low in your ear. And the dizzy, overwhelming sweetness of being seen, known, and wanted—all for the first time.

Mitali Perkins

Mitali Perkins is the author of several books for teens, including *Monsoon Summer* (2006), *Secret Keeper* (2010), *Bamboo People* (2010), and the First Daughter books. She and the guy in this letter went their separate ways during college, where she met and married the love of her life. The Perkins family lives in Massachusetts with a chubby black Labrador. Visit her at MitaliPerkins.com.

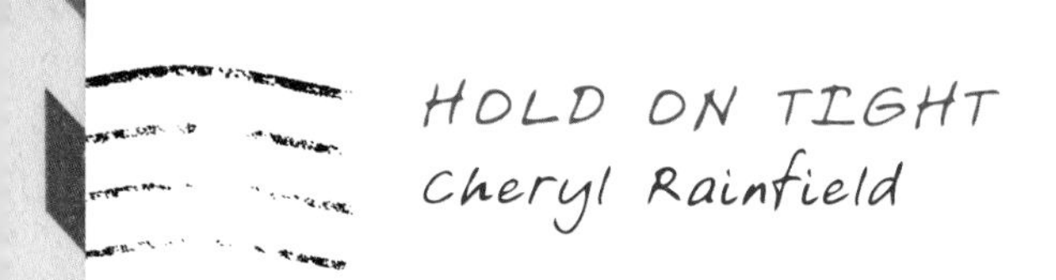

HOLD ON TIGHT
Cheryl Rainfield

Dear Teen Me,

I know you dream of escape, of being rescued, of never being hurt again. I know you think your pain will never end, and sometimes you don't know how to go on. And I know you think about killing yourself. You're good with blades, and you know that you could do it. But something stops you. And that something is good: It's hope. Hope, tenacity, and your fighting spirit.

I know that when your pain feels unbearable, when every second seems like torture, you cut yourself in secret, then carefully hide the evidence beneath long sleeves. But you wish someone would see the truth and ask "why?" You wish someone could see past your parents' facades, their "protectiveness," and their tight smiles, and see how cruel they really are.

I know it seems like it will never end—the rape, the torture—and so you push it down as hard as you can and try to forget, but fragments keep slicing into your mind. Somehow, you're sure that remembering is the only way to get safe. And you're right. Remembering and telling your story is the key to your safety.

You *will* escape. You'll run away from home, and when they find you again, you'll have to endure even more abuse. But you'll keep building up your inner strength so that you can find a way to break away again and again and again. Each and every time that you cut off contact with your abusers, you liberate yourself a little bit more, until you are finally and completely free.

You'll find a good therapist, one who gives you empathy, compassion, and love. She will be a lifeline for you, and you're right to seek her support. It's too hard to do it alone. All those experiences and your own intuition will help you figure out exactly who you can trust. You'll fight your abusers' attempts to break you down by creating your own counter messages, and by finding other people who will appreciate and support you. You'll break through your abusers' mind control, lies, and threats, and you'll find your voice in writing. You'll write books! And they'll reach other teens who need them. You will touch lives.

I know you feel like you can't hang on. I know you feel like you can't survive. But you will, and you'll be glad that you did. You'll have moments of quiet happiness, and later, joy. You'll find true friends who treasure you. It won't always hurt like this. It won't always be like it is right now. The pain will lessen.

Stop hating yourself. The hatred doesn't belong to you. It belongs to the ones who torture you. Try to let it go, and to be gentle with yourself. Try not to hurt yourself. You don't deserve it. Believe in yourself—in your vision and your goodness—and trust yourself. You know what you need. Just keep holding on. Good things are coming, I promise.

So keep hold of your strength. You are so much stronger than you know. Keep hold of your compassion, your intuition, and your intelligence. They can't take those things away from you. Keep writing, keep creating art, keep reading, and keep finding your way through the darkness. You'll make a good life for yourself. And you *will* find safety, happiness, and love. So hang on until then, my girl.

Cheryl Rainfield

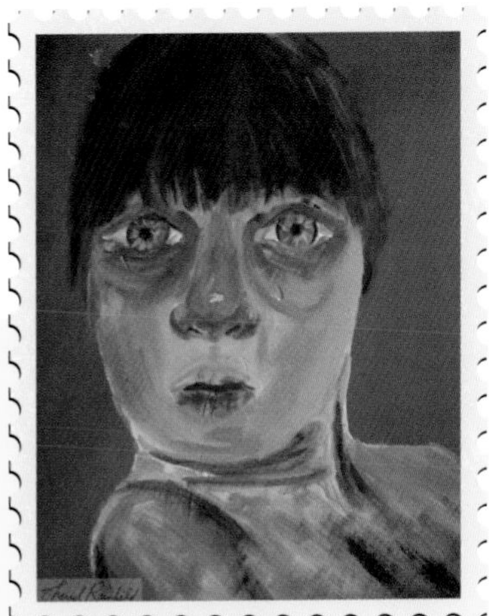

Cheryl Rainfield is the author of *Hunted* (2011) and *Scars* (2010), a Top 10 YALSA Quick Pick for Reluctant Readers and a Governor General Literary Award Finalist. Visit CherylRainfield.com, Twitter.com/CherylRainfield, and Facebook.com/CherylRainfield.

It won't be easy for you to move on.

Closing yourself off isn't the answer, but it will feel like the safest choice.

Choices you'll regret for the rest of your life.

Don't feel bad about all that time alone, most of it will actually end up being productive.
(Maybe give up that bass guitar.)
The more you focus your attention on writing and drawing, the better!
BRISTOL
Get Caller ID, so you can better avoid distractions.
RING RING RING
RAPIDOGRAPH
WHITE OUT
COMIX
COMIC BOOK
I've decided not to stay in America, so I think YOU should take this.
MINI-COMIC
SVA
COLLEGE APPLICATION
Once you leave high school, a whole new world will open up to you.
SCHOOL OF VISUAL ARTS
SELF PUBLISHING 101
JUNIOR YEAR
INTERNSHIP PROGRAM
EDITORIAL ASSISTANT
DC COMICS

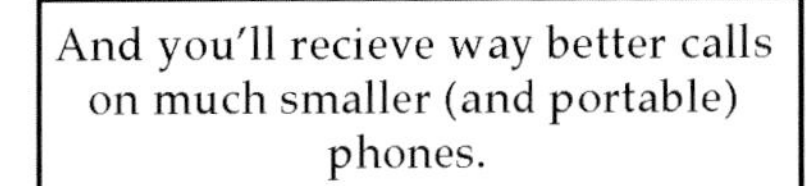

Dave Roman is the creator of *Astronaut Academy: Zero Gravity* (2011), and has written several graphic novels including *Jax Epoch and the Quicken Forbidden* (cocreated with John Green and self-published in 2003, while they were students at the School of Visual Arts) and *Teen Boat!* (2012). Dave was a comics editor at *Nickelodeon Magazine* for eleven years. He collaborated with his wife, Raina Telgemeier, on *X-Men: Misfits* (2009), which was a *New York Times* best-seller. His website is YayTime.com.

STOP OBSESSING, KISS THAT GUY, AND PARTY LIKE IT'S 1999

Jess Rothenberg

Dear Teen Me,

Greetings from the future! So I know you're super busy with studying, college apps, tennis practice, memorizing your lines for *Peter Pan*, backing your new car into a tree, trying (and failing) to tame that totally frizz-tastic hair of yours, and watching *Titanic* for the eightieth time—but I have to ask you for a small favor. (Hint: The favor involves backing away from the "I ♥ Leonardo DiCaprio" chat room for just a quick second.)

So being that I am you—except ten or twelve years from now—I wanted to pop in with a few pointers on how to make the next phase of life a little less painful and a little more fun. I'm not going to give you ALL the answers, since (a) that would be cheating and (b) I'm still searching for most of them myself, but there are a few specific words of wisdom I'd love to share.

➧ 1. Never, ever try cutting your own bangs. So there's this movie called *500 Days of Summer* that will come out in 2009 and make you/every girl in the universe want bangs more than anything. But trust me, just because bangs look amazing on Zooey Deschanel does NOT mean they will look good on you. When you make that fateful snip, you'll discover the horrible truth: You have not one, but TWO cowlicks on either side of your forehead! No amount of product will save you, Teen Jess. And you will spend YEARS waiting for that shit to grow out. So do us both a favor and back away from the scissors! You've been warned.

➧ 2. Shake it like a Polaroid picture. Take advantage of your teenage hotness! Dance it up! Sing it up! Live it up! Flaunt that bikini and buy that hot pink miniskirt you've been eyeing at T. J. Maxx. It all looks amazing on you, so show off that gravity-free bod while you can! In a few years when you're slaving/daydreaming in an office cubicle, you'll so wish you had.

➧ 3. Sha-la-la-la-la-la, don't be shy, go on and kiss that guy! (Like in *The Little Mermaid*, but reversed!) Don't be scared of guys, Teen Jess. You may have spent years at an all-girls' school, but I'm here to report boys aren't all that different from your average household pest (hungry, hairy, and helpless)! And trust me, they're JUST as scared of you as you are of them.

- 4. Party like it's 1999. When you move to New York, a wise person will tell you: RSVP yes to EVERYTHING. *So* true! Unless you're literally dying of malaria, never skip out on a party—even one you think will be lame. Why? Because you never know who you're going to meet! I won't spoil the surprise, but believe me, one of those parties will change your life more than you could possibly imagine...in a good way!
- 5. Stop obsessing. It's totally normal to worry about what other people think of you. But I swear, the only people whose opinions *truly* matter are your best friends and family. Forget about the rest! In a few years, high school will feel like forever ago. The world is *enormous*, and you've got lots of awesome adventures ahead of you. Sure, you'll make some mistakes along the way. (Thank goodness, because otherwise life would get pretty boring!) So in those stressful moments, just take a deep breath, chillax, and do your best to ENJOY THE RIDE. You'll be glad you did. :)

Jess Rothenberg grew up in Charleston, South Carolina, graduated from Vassar College, and spent most of her twenties editing books for teens and middle-grade readers (like *New York Times* best-sellers *Vampire Academy*, *Strange Angels*, and *I am a Genius of Unspeakable Evil & I Want to Be Your Class President*, to name a few). She lives in Brooklyn, where she writes full-time, dances interpretively, and dreams of one day owning a sheepdog named Leo. *The Catastrophic History of You and Me* (2012) is her first novel. Visit JessRothenberg.com.

Q and A:

"Summer camp, after a bonfire."

Elizabeth Miles

~

"In a plastic 'cozy cottage' from Toys 'R' Us in my backyard. (I closed the plastic windows!)"

Jessica Burkhart

~

"Basement. Spin the Bottle. Kim H."

Geoff Herbach

~

"My first kiss was when I was 15 and at a roller rink. It was cheesy and amazing...I was majorly crushing on the guy. The kiss didn't happen on the rink though—he was playing a video game and I just walked up and did it. I know how to make the magic happen, people."

Rhonda Stapleton

~

"Stuffed between smelly overcoats in a closet at a party."

Sean Beaudoin

~

"Church camp!"

Sarah Ockler

~

"In my bedroom while watching wrestling on TV. My brother kept interrupting because he wanted to watch wrestling with the guy I had over. But I wanted to kiss!"

Miranda Kenneally

~

"In the front seat of a pick-up truck—being careful of the stick shift. No pun intended."

Bethany Hegedus

~

"Behind my cabin at sleep-away camp—where my entire bunk watched (and cheered) through the whole humiliating thing, 1994"

Jess Rothenberg

~

"Backstage. I was wearing makeup to make me look like an old woman."

Hannah Moskowitz

~

"In a closet."

Marke Bieschke

~

"My first real kiss—a kiss with a girl I both cared about and was attracted to—didn't take place until my freshman year in college. It was in the front seat of my '59 Plymouth just before I said goodnight after a date at the movies. And, no, I am not going to tell you her name."

Joseph Bruchac

~

"I never kiss and tell"

Riley Carney

~

ALL ROADS LEAD SOMEWHERE

Jennifer Rush

Dear Teen Me,

In the fall of 2001, your friend will call you late at night and ask you to go for a ride. She doesn't have a destination. She's just bored and wants to hang out.

Here's my first bit of advice: *Go.*

Around 2:00 am, your friend will take the highway back into town. The road stretches on for twenty miles, but you know that somewhere on that road your cousin owns a house. To pass the time, you look for his vehicle in the slide of headlights. Since he just recently moved there, you're mostly curious to see what the place looks like.

Ten minutes from the main road, when you've given up the search, you'll see flashing red and blue lights.

Here's my next bit of advice: *Sit up.*

There's an ambulance in a dirt driveway. A cop car. You twist around as you pass.

"Something crazy's going down there," your friend says.

Don't look away.

An hour later, back at home, the phone will ring. "I need to talk to your mom," your aunt says in a voice so strained you can barely hear her.

"She's sleeping—"

"Wake her up. Please."

You rush down the hallway. Shake your mom awake. Hand her the phone. You step back and wait. Wait. And wait. It'll only be a few seconds, but it'll seem like forever.

Just when you think you can't stand it any longer, your mom will let out a choked sob and somehow you'll know this is connected to the cop car, to the ambulance. You'll feel it in your heart and in your gut.

"Chad's dead," your mom will say. Your cousin. *That house was his.*

He committed suicide, you'll learn. He was your favorite and you let him know it. And maybe it seemed like a joke to the family, but it was true. You adored him. He was smart. And funny. And happy. Wasn't he? He was so much more than you ever thought you could be.

Why would he do it? you'll wonder. *Why?* This is a question that will never have an answer, but you can't stop asking it.

The next day, you'll be lost and numb and everyone will be crying and you can't take the crying. Call your friend Wes. *Call him.* He'll help you escape.

At dinnertime, you'll realize you haven't eaten all day. At the fast-food place, Wes will know the boy behind the counter. You won't catch his name. He'll give you extra fries. On a day like this, the fries mean more than they normally would.

Remember him. It'll be a hazy memory, but keep it tucked away.

Three months later, a boy will come into the Laundromat where you work. He'll ask you out. *Say yes.*

It will take you a few weeks, several dates, many hours spent on the phone, before you realize he was the boy behind the counter. The one who gave you the fries. That boy will become your husband.

Somehow, on one of the worst nights of your life, you'll meet the most *important* person in your life. Fate may seem a silly notion, but sometimes, tiny, inconspicuous moments will connect to something bigger, something profound. So my last bit of advice is this: *Take nothing for granted. Keep your heart and your eyes open.* You never know when you'll meet someone extraordinary. Or, even if it's for a second in the dark, in a car on the highway, you'll get your only chance to say good-bye.

Jennifer Rush

Jennifer Rush is the author of the forthcoming young adult thriller *Altered.* She currently lives in a little 1930s house in a small town on the shoreline of Lake Michigan with her husband, the fabulously supportive J.V., and her two crazy kids.

SMILE!

Amy Kathleen Ryan

Dear Teen Me,

I know you hate to be told what to do with your face. Elderly men in particular love telling you to smile—for which you reward them with a sarcastic smirk. Good work. They should mind their own business. But since I'm you, and your face is mine, I have every right to make this suggestion: Slap a grin on your mug.

You know how you never get asked out on dates? That's because you lurch through the hallways of your school with your head down as if you were ducking enemy fire.

I can't blame you. High school isn't easy. You've got all types—from motorheads to eggheads to potheads—crammed into a single building at high density, and you have to get through the day without erupting into civil war. I have news for you, too: Adults wouldn't be able to do it. In adulthood, people have self-sorted into pockets of like-minded compadres. The computer geeks work together at Microsoft, the debate members have all joined law firms, and the drama kids are launching off-off-Broadway plays in Minneapolis. So don't listen to adults telling you these are the best years of your life. It gets infinitely better when you can choose what you do, where, and with whom. But until that day comes, smile!

I'm not saying you should be one of those plastic, ever-chipper girls who bounce through the hallway swinging their ponytails behind them like bullwhips. These girls will grow up to be real estate agents, politicians, and PTA presidents. Their smiles will become like debit cards, earning them professional capital, but depleting them in the soul department.

Nonetheless, there are occasions when it would be eminently appropriate for you to smile. For instance, you know that cute guy in the leather jacket who was ogling you at the football game? And you know how you were so nervous you could barely glance in his direction? When you did look at him, it was oh so casually, as though your eye was actually drawn to the overboiled hotdogs behind him, and you just happened to look at his manly shoulders by accident. Did it never once occur to you that you could actually *smile* at him? Give him a little invitation? A little facial tic that says, "Hi. I am receptive. Please initiate." If you'd managed to contort your frown a mere thirty degrees upward, he might be dating you and your fuzzy 1980s perm right now (instead of that girl with the bubble butt and colored contacts).

Because here's the thing I don't think you realize: It is actually possible for a guy to be attracted to you. No, you're not the prettiest girl in school. And you're definitely not the most popular. But that doesn't mean that some nice, cute guy couldn't notice you. And if you encouraged him with a friendly grin, he might be able to overcome his nervousness enough to say hi. And then you might have a date for homecoming instead of being forced to hang out on the bleachers with your wallflower girlfriends mouthing the lyrics to "Forever Young."

You won't be, you know. Your looks will fade, and you'll spend money on creams and tinctures to try and buy a few more minutes of youthfulness. That's what I do now every night; I scrub away dead skin cells by whatever means necessary. I'm trying to look like you. That's because you're beautiful. *All* teenage girls are beautiful. Your eyes are clear. Your skin is wrinkle-free. You're energetic and lovely by virtue of your gorgeous, enviable youth. So don't waste it. Pull your face up out of its foxhole. Take a chance on the world. Smile.

AKR

Amy Kathleen Ryan is the author of *Vibes* (2010), *Zen and Xander Undone* (2011), and *Glow* (2011)—the first book in the Sky Chasers series. She lives in Colorado with her family.

SING IT OUT

Tom Ryan

Dear Teen Me,

Let me get this out of the way first: You're gay. And in the end, you'll come out. And yes, eventually it does get better. Much better.

But let's just say that it doesn't happen overnight. In fact, there's a whole hell of a lot you'll have to deal with in the meantime before you're able to admit who you really are.

That's what I want to talk about now: the meantime.

First up: Don't stop singing. Please.

You love singing. I know it. I know that the first thing you'll do after you get your license is grab your favorite mix tape, pop it in the tape deck, and drive around by yourself singing along (at the top of your mother-freaking lungs) to Fleetwood Mac, Aerosmith, and Roxette.

You love dancing too, right? Jumping up and down and feeling like a superstar in the movie of your life?

You like to bake cookies and decorate cakes. You like sassy female comedians. You like to watch figure skating. You write poetry about sunsets over the ocean. Do you get where I'm going with this?

Yep. You love a whole bunch of supergay shit.

And that's okay, despite what the voice has to say.

You know exactly what I'm talking about. The nasty little voice in the back of your head that tells you to rein it in, to try acting straight. The voice that tells you that the things you love and the thoughts you think make you worthless—an embarrassment. The voice that says you should be ashamed of yourself.

Worst of all, the voice will tell you, day and night, that if you don't watch your step, then people will start to see who you really are.

But there are also going to be times when you can't help yourself. When you let yourself get up onstage and belt out a tune for an audience. When you bust out your disco moves at the school dance because *somebody* has to do the Bee Gees justice. When you come to school bursting with the latest Hollywood gossip because it's just too juicy to not talk about. When you buy that sweater at Le Chateau, because you *have to*—I mean, come on, it's the *perfect* shade of green!

The voice is going to tell you to hold it all in—and more often than not, the voice will win out over your instincts. But sometimes you're going to tell the voice to shut the eff up, because you can't help it. You can't help doing the things you want to do. Sometimes you just can't help being who you are.

And those times are going to be the best times. When you don't care what people think, when you let yourself do the things you want to do, with the people you love. They're going to be the best times because you are better at being yourself than you are at being anyone else.

So please, promise me something...When you feel like singing, just do it. Lift up your head, close your eyes, open your lungs, and sing. Sing so loud and so long that the voice has no choice but to shut up and listen.

Eventually, you won't even remember what it sounds like.

Tom Ryan

Tom Ryan was born and raised in Inverness, Nova Scotia. His first novel, *Way to Go* (2012), was recently published. He can be found online at TomWroteThat.com.

I'M NOT GOING TO GIVE YOU ANY GOOD ADVICE

Leila Sales

Dear Teen Me,

You're probably hoping that I'm writing to you—from *the future*—with words of advice, sage wisdom I have picked up over my years as an adult which will somehow save you from all embarrassing and depressing situations. I should do that, shouldn't I? It would be really nice of me to help you be a more well adjusted person.

The trouble with that is, when I think of advice I could give you, I mostly come up with things for you *not* to do.

For example, when the boy you've had a crush on for two years rests his elbow on your shoulder, *do not* respond by saying, "Aren't you a little short for that?" Yes, that will remove his arm, but it will also remove any chance you might have had of going out with him.

Do not write long letters to every girl in your bunk at camp, or to every member of your graduating class, in which you explain to them how much you care about them and explain how they can still improve themselves. This is weird, and nobody will appreciate it. You are actually not an expert on other people's character flaws. Furthermore, writing fifty letters is a huge time investment, and you could probably spend those hours doing something more useful, like learning how to cook (which you still do not know how to do, sorry).

Do not go on a self-loathing spree after you get rejected from your four top-choice colleges. It's not because you're worthless and unappreciated; it's because getting into college is hard.

Do not pull out in front of that school bus when there's a police car directly behind you. That's a one-hundred-dollar ticket, Teen Me. You could use that hundred dollars, if you still had it today. You could buy yourself a new iPod. (Teen Me, iPods are this amazing technology that let you carry around *thousands* of songs instead of just a few CDs. I mean it. The future is a crazy place.)

Anyway. I could go on. You make a lot of mistakes as a teenager, it's true, and you make some enemies as well. But here's the thing: I don't *actually* want you to avoid those mistakes. Because then you would have nothing to write about.

Even if I could instruct you on how to get through high school without offending a single one of your classmates, without scaring off a single boy, without angering any of your teachers—even then, I wouldn't do it. Because each time you ate lunch alone in the library or totally botched a stage kiss, you were giving yourself the materials you now need as a novelist.

Eventually every one of your missteps, and every person who wouldn't give you the time of day, will make their way into your books. And teenagers all over the world will read those books, and some will even say things like, "I love this book. Leila Sales seems really cool." I'm serious. If you give it enough time, *teenagers will think you are cool*. It won't be *while* you're a teenager, but still.

So do exactly what you're doing. Make every mistake you're making, but also learn from them, remember them, and use them.

Two exceptions to that advice:

Do not be so bitchy to your dad.

And *do not* blow-dry the life out of your hair every day. Your hair is curly, and it looks good curly. Forcing it to be something that it's not isn't fooling anybody.

Other than those two things, just carry on as you were. Mistakes and all.

Leila

Leila Sales grew up outside of Boston and graduated from the University of Chicago. She is the author of the novels *Mostly Good Girls* (2010) and *Past Perfect* (2011). When not writing, she spends most of her time thinking about chocolate, kittens, dancing, sleeping, and receiving unsolicited text messages from strangers (which you can read about on her blog, The Leila Texts). Leila lives and writes in Brooklyn.

FRIENDS IN DARK PLACES

Cynthia Leitich Smith

Dear Teen Me,

You've had enough of the quarters game in the kitchen, the "Pink Floyd" album in the rec room, and the whispers and stares everywhere else. A girl on your high school newspaper staff just told you he was here. You have to get away. You're not ready to see him yet.

It's more than that actually. You're not ready for everyone else to dissect how you two interact...or don't. Maybe that sounds superficial, but this is social theater, and you're the leading lady of the week. You're not about to let them see you crumble.

What are you doing here anyway? You barely know the girl whose parents (currently out of town) own this place. Maybe your best friend had a point: Moping at home wasn't helping, but offering yourself up as the focus of tonight's drama wasn't the best idea either.

For the first time, a boyfriend has told you that he doesn't want you anymore. You've been together for months. You've gone on countless variations of his preferred date: dinner at a chain restaurant followed by the yogurt shop or miniature golf. You've been to church with his family, and he's celebrated the holidays with yours. Your parents like him, especially your dad. They connect over football.

Was it because you're a virgin? Is that why he dumped you? He never pressured. He never even brought it up. But that's what your gut says.

In your suburban high school, it seems like a cheerleader gets pregnant every single year. You're horrified by how people turn their backs on those girls, and you're determined that it won't happen to you. Could he sense that?

The split-level house is crowded. You squeeze past drunken kids to reach the second floor. Someone asks if you know he's there, and you pretend not to hear. Couples are making out in the bathroom and in the bedrooms you pass. You slip into the master, where coats and purses are piled on the bed, and shut the door.

You need a few moments to pull yourself together. It's already late. You consider hiding out there until your friends are ready to leave.

Then the door opens. Of all people, it's the girl who's been bullying you from the day you first moved to this district, back in fourth grade. She spray-painted the word "Bitch" on your driveway, and mocked your discount-store clothes.

That's why you're a cheerleader. You tried out for the wardrobe that came with it. Who would've guessed you'd take away her spot on the squad?

After that, she faded into the background. Until tonight. Has she been waiting for the opportunity to attack? You feel exposed, vulnerable.

"You're too good for him," she announces, and you assume it's a trick.

You brace yourself for the punch line. You brace yourself to *be* the punch line, like you had been for many years before. But it doesn't come. She's sincere.

Has the world turned upside down?

"Why are you, of all people, being nice to me?" you demand with more spirit than you've ever shown her, toe-to-toe, before.

She blames the past on jealousy. She tells you how much you wow her.

It's a small miracle. If she can change, then you will, too. No more hiding. You go downstairs to confront the boy. To ask what went wrong.

Years later, you won't care enough to remember what he said.

In the end, that won't be the conversation that mattered.

Cynthia Leitich Smith

Cynthia Leitich Smith is the *New York Times* best-selling author of the Tantalize series, award-winning books for younger readers and numerous short stories. She went to high school in the suburbs of Kansas City and earned degrees in journalism and law before deciding to write fiction full-time. Today Cynthia makes her home in Austin, Texas, with her husband, author Greg Leitich Smith, and four feisty writer cats. Visit her at CynthiaLeitichSmith.com.

FINDING HIM

Jessica Spotswood

Dear Teen Me,

You are a truly whimsical being. You wish upon a star every Christmas Eve (and on fireworks during the Fourth of July). You read Victoria Holt and Judith McNaught and *Gone with the Wind*, over and over again. You've never been kissed, but you write sprawling historical romance novels filled with flirtatious banter and spirited, thinly veiled Scarlett O'Haras.

You want to fall in love.

All of your best friends are dating. You're simultaneously envious of and annoyed by their constant PDAs. When their romances are going well they don't need you; but when they fall apart, your friends get all devastated and depressed and make very questionable decisions. Their entire sense of self-worth seems hinged on these relationships, and you don't ever want to be like that. You swear that when you fall in love, you won't lose yourself.

Your stepmom says you're the type of girl who will marry her first serious boyfriend, and you know what? She's right.

It will take a while for you to find him, though. Right now you're going through a succession of crushes on boys who only see you as a friend, and who therefore don't think it's at all awkward to confide in you about their crushes on other girls. It's mortifying. But in college you'll make some amazing girlfriends—the kind who won't drop you when they get boyfriends or husbands or jobs or anything. You'll make out with a few boys. You'll also have more wild crushes, which will make you feel small and stupid when they are not reciprocated. You'll become as cynical as you are capable of being (which is not very, because you're inherently optimistic). You will want to murder anyone who calls you *cute*, because *cute* seems naïve.

The boy who will become our husband, the Playwright—he is brilliant and witty and he never says what you expect him to. It's maddening; you can't decide whether you want to kiss him or kick him. When you're almost twenty, you'll be in a play together, and after every rehearsal and performance you'll stand outside the theater talking together, and your friends will suspect long before you do that you like him. I won't tell you how you finally realize that you're interested in each other. Some things are lovely surprises.

The Playwright never makes you feel small or stupid or calls you *cute* in that condescending way. In fact, he once tells you that you're like Cruella de Vil and the Dalmatians rolled into one person. You will be bizarrely delighted by this.

You will fall in love, but you won't lose yourself. You won't be one of those couples who are attached at the hip, who always speak in *we*'s. He will have rehearsals, see experimental plays that you hate, and be mildly obsessed with fantasy football. You will go on writing retreats and girls' spa weekends and have a standing Tuesday dinner date with your best friend. You'll still be an independent girl, but you can be braver and stronger and better once you're confident that you are loved.

Teen Me, I know we're not very good at patience. But he's worth waiting for.

Jessica Spotswood

Jessica Spotswood is the author of *Born Wicked* (2012), Book 1 of The Cahill Witch Chronicles. She lives in Washington, DC, with her playwright husband and a very cuddly cat named Monkey. She loves theater, tea, cardamom cookies, the color pink, twirly dresses, and the sound of bells chiming the hour. Jess is never happier than when she's immersed in a good story. (Swoony kissing scenes are her favorite.)

BOYS BOYS BOYS
Erika Stalder

Dear Teen Me,

Let's talk about boys. I know, I know—you think the topic is overhyped and undervalued. And you're annoyed that seemingly all the chicks around you are consumed—*consumed*!—by boy stuff. I really can't blame you for thinking "Gawd—enough already!" What with your best friend dating a twenty-five-year-old gangster with jailhouse tattoos and a gunplay fetish (not to mention a thing for MUCH younger, virginal girls—gross!), and your carpool buddy who rhapsodizes on and *on* about her boy exploits...It's pretty exhausting.

And of course it doesn't help that your first date was with a guy who drove a windowless van (which he borrowed), and who didn't bring enough money to even cover his *own* tab. Or that most of the hotties in your tiny school act like dopey surfer brahs who consume beerios (yes, that's Cheerios in beer—ugh) for breakfast. But humor me.

Try to be nicer to the boys in your school. Even though the boy frontier is tumultuous, embarrassingly underexplored, and sometimes a downright hassle, high school guys are trying to get by just like you. They're worried about whether their V cards have surpassed the socially acceptable use-by date. And they've all got that girl they desperately want to talk to but are terrified of approaching, just because they might be rejected. And despite the amount of misplaced innuendo and attaboying they engage in, these guys *can* be sincere. Sometimes, when a guy tells you that you look pretty, he means it, and you should simply thank him instead of *knowing* that he's messing with you and flashing your signature "don't eff with me" glare.

And for God's sake—when you're at that post-lip-sync party with your crush, make a move! I know you're all worried about ruining your friendship with the guy, but after high school, you'll never talk to him again—so that friendship isn't as important as you think. What's more, when you see him a year or so outta high school, you won't even think he's cute anymore—so get him while the gettin's good! Not only will he likely go for a little action, but making the first move with a guy will be great practice in gutsiness, semicalculated risk taking, and, most importantly, seeing the sweet side of the male species while you're still in high school. Because as you'll see, even just a year out of high school, the menfolk are awesome.

Speaking of which, I've got a few highlights for you: There's an amazing mix-tape-making photographer you're about to meet. He whisks you off to this secret, mountaintop location and treats you to the perfect picnic. You sit together up there, looking up at the stars, and even though it's definitely the stuff that rom-coms are made of, it still feels magical and authentic. There's also this bass-playing skater guy who takes the time to teach you to kick-kick-push, who doesn't make fun of you when you eat pavement, *and* who doctors you up after you scrape the hell out of your leg trying to barrel down a hill. The guys in your life just keep getting better and better as your life goes on, and all you have to do to access their awesomeness is just let down your guard a bit. Good luck, and enjoy it!

E. Stalder

Erika Stalder is a Cali-based journalist who has penned five nonfiction books for teens, including *The Date Book* (2007), *Fashion 101: A Crash Course in Clothing* (2008), and *The Look Book: 50 Iconic Beauties and How to Achieve Their Signature Styles* (2011)—all with Zest Books. She has written articles for magazines and websites including *Wired, Gizmodo, Missbehave, Planet* and *MTV Style.* She writes Dear Erika, a weekly advice column for teens in conjunction with ABC Family's hit show *Secret Life of the American Teen*, and is FINALLY working to realize her teenage dream with the launch of an online magazine for teens at ErikaStalder.com.

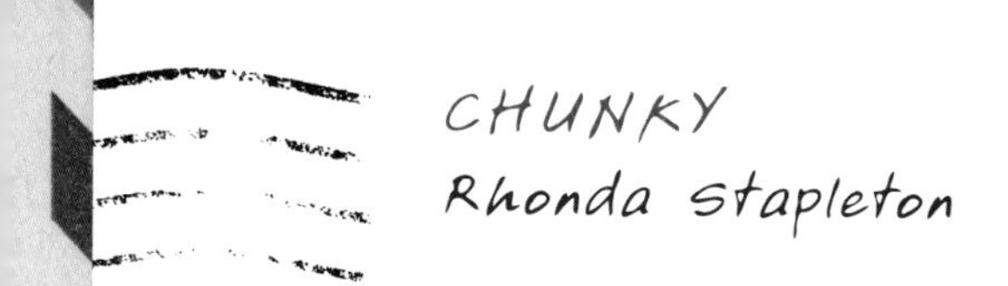

CHUNKY

Rhonda Stapleton

Dear Teen Me,

Looking a little chunky, aren't ya?

Before that guy in junior English class said that to you, you'd had some fleeting worries about your thighs being a little too big. Your hips just a touch too curvy. But you'd just grown into a real bra size the summer before. You felt feminine, confident, strong.

Right up to that comment.

Those words are going to haunt you for a long time. Every time you look at yourself in the mirror, you'll hear his voice: "Looking a little chunky, aren't ya?"

Not that you want to admit to yourself or to anyone else that one stupid guy has the power to hurt you like that. Especially one you had a crush on—a fleeting emotion that crashed and burned point-two seconds after he said that to you. But they're just words, right? That's what you told yourself that day as you bit back the sting, blinked away the tears, slipped into your seat, and stared blindly ahead, your cheeks burning hot with humiliation. They're just words, and words can't hurt.

You never saw yourself the same way again after that, though. Your lens was broken.

I look back on you, remembering the way you studied every inch of your thighs, your butt, your belly in the mirror day after day, sucking in, wishing you were skinnier. And I feel sick that your view of yourself became skewed because of what one (thoughtless) person thought of you.

Because after that, you didn't dress for fun, for flair. You dressed to accentuate the good and conceal the bad.

It wasn't about personal statement. It was camouflage. It was illusion.

What's even worse is that you weren't *chunky*. You were healthy. You were curvy. You were attractive. But none of that mattered, because someone who didn't care about you or your feelings blurted out one a sentence he probably forgot about five minutes later.

Not you, though. You lost almost all of your power and your self-confidence shortly after that. And you didn't stop there—even into adulthood you were surrounded by images of beautiful women on TV, in movies, magazines, real life. Because beauty is a girl's greatest asset, isn't it? Perfect face, perfect body. Perfect soul. And you longed, you ached to look like them.

You have a daughter now. She's fifteen—a sophomore. She has a free spirit, dresses how she pleases, doesn't give a damn what others think of her. She's healthy, she's curvy, she's attractive. But deep down you worry that some stupid boy is going to say something to mess that up.

You can't change the cruel things people say. But don't ever, *ever* forget that beauty goes beyond what you look like. Your beauty is in your heart. You care deeply about others. You smile freely. You're generous with your time and spirit. There isn't a damn thing anyone else can say about you that will change that.

Embrace your curves. They reflect your unique femininity. Your body is amazing! It will carry you to New York City, New Orleans, Oahu, San Francisco. It will bear your stresses, bear your children. It gives the most amazing hugs. It loves belly dancing, booty grinding, doing the sprinkler. It loves to walk, to hold hands, to kick leaves, and swim through big piles of snow.

No one has power over you. Not now, not ever. So please, step away from the mirror and step back into your life. You'll thank me for it later.

Rhonda Stapleton

Rhonda Stapleton has a bachelor's degree in English, creative writing, and a master's degree in English. She is the author of the teen romantic comedy trilogy *Stupid Cupid* (2009), *Flirting with Disaster* (2010), and *Pucker Up* (2010). You can find these books in the new three-in-one bind-up, *Struck* (2011). Rhonda also works as an acquisitions and developmental editor for Carina Press. To learn more about her and her books, visit RhondaStapleton.com.

KEEPING QUIET

Mariko Tamaki

Dear Teen Me,

You're fifteen years old, and you want to die.

Just so you know, not a lot of people know this about you. People see you with your book, sitting in the windowsill. They see you writing poetry in your poetry binder. They see your picture in the yearbook, bangs in your face, slouched in the back row. But that's all they see.

No one knows how sad you are. Your parents don't even know you're sad at all, mostly because you avoid them—preferring to snack on cereal and soy sauce (separately) in your room.

Of course, you have your reasons for keeping to yourself. Girls are so mean in grade school. Later on you'll marvel at this phenomenon, watching a new generation of teenagers from a safe distance, while teaching creative writing. But at fifteen, this cruelty feels overwhelmingly close. And you feel so incredibly vulnerable.

What I'm trying to say is that yes, it obviously makes sense to try and avoid them, to stay hidden in the camouflage of a shadow. To keep quiet.

But here's the thing. You keep quiet instead of expressing yourself (which is only a little ironic because you're also a huge fan of Madonna). You keep quiet instead of saying things you think are funny, because you're afraid people won't get the joke and will think you're weird. You keep your heart tucked into your sleeve instead of being honest about the things and the people (the girls) that you love, because being open about this stuff seems like a surefire invitation for attack.

But this is not a solution. It's a problem, and it's what makes you start to think about suicide—about getting away for good.

And let me tell you something, as soon as you stop being quiet, as soon as you stop hiding, and hiding who you are, things will change.

Before this happens, though, you're going to experience a real crisis. You'll spend some time in a hospital, and that won't be any fun at all. You'll be diagnosed with depression. And it will seem like an insurmountable diagnosis. But it's won't be. Instead, by hitting rock bottom at fifteen, you'll quickly learn how silly it is to be afraid.

After the hospital you'll suddenly feel like you have nothing to lose. Hiding your true self will seem like a ridiculous task, because everyone will now have PROOF that you are different. You'll be legitimately, REALLY, crazy. Everyone at school will know you had to be admitted to the hospital. The "why" will vary according to which particular rumor people choose to believe. So, you'll think, "Who cares? So I'm nuts. SO WHAT?"

First you'll find your look—a punk rock, artsy, goth-type thing. You'll discover the joys of eyeliner as lipstick. You'll wear little old lady dresses and striped tights. You'll buy ten-hole purple Doc Martens and wear them to bed because you love them so much. You'll discover the joys of being the strangest person in the room. You'll dye your hair purple.

Three years later you'll go to university and meet and fall in love with a girl who dyes her hair pink.

And, just so you know, even though no one gets your jokes in high school, people will TOTALLY (mostly) get them later on.

As your future self, I can make this promise: Things will TOTALLY get better. Have a little faith in yourself. So stop hiding. Stop being quiet. Be brave.

Mariko Tamaki is a Toronto-based performer and the author of the award-winning graphic novel *Skim* (2010). Mariko's upcoming works include a novel about freshman year, *(You) Set Me on Fire*, and a comic book, *Awago Beach Babies*, co-created with Jillian Tamaki. Mariko still wears dresses from Goodwill and purple Docs, and still loves to dye her hair purple. Visit MarikoTamaki.Blogspot.com.

STOLEN JEANS, SMOKE RINGS, AND SELF-ESTEEM

Don Tate

Dear Teen Me,

Hey there, Donny Tate! I'm sorry to interrupt while you paint. I know how focused you are in art mode, but we need to talk. I am you, thirty years later. My hair is grayer, my face is fuller, my pants are a few sizes larger. But I'm still here—*we're* still here—alive and kicking in 2012. We're lucky, though, 'cause you almost messed it up for the both of us.

You sit there at seventeen-years-old in your high school art class. All decked out in your Playboy shirt, Levi's jeans, penny loafer shoes. We dressed to impress. But something's wrong with this picture, and you and I both know it. You stole those jeans (...and the shirt...and the shoes). And you smell like an ashtray after cutting gym class to smoke cigarettes in the parking lot with your boys.

I'm not trying to out you, but if I'm going to help you get on the right track, I need to be real.

I'm writing this letter to give you a piece of advice—something you and I will learn the hard way, after many years of bad decisions: You don't need to prove anything to anyone but God and yourself.

Don't worry, I'm not getting all church-boy on you, so wipe the attitude off your face. (You're just like your daughter—the one you've already conceived at seventeen and don't even know about yet.) Listen, you spend way too much time trying to impress others. For example, that stuff you stole—you didn't need it. You have two jobs. You stole to impress your friends. And they were impressed. So much so, they pressed you to steal stuff for them, too. Clothes, electronics, hair care products. Whatever they wanted, you got it for them. But where were those "friends" when the police showed up and you got fined for shoplifting?

Please know I'm not judging you. High school is tough, and your home life is too. Especially after mom and dad got divorced. You want to be liked by your peers. You want to be looked up to, held in high esteem. But the most important man in your life—our dad!—dragged your self-esteem through the mud. He didn't accept you as the artist you were. He wanted a sports star. He

didn't like your brown skin. He wanted a light-skinned kid with straight hair. He drank a lot and said a lot of really mean things. I get that. I understand.

But there's something else *you* need to understand : Your mom, she loves you. Your grandma and grandpa do, too. Your three little brothers all look up to you and love you. In fact—and you'll find this hard to believe—your dad, he loves you too. He just doesn't know how to show it, because he didn't have a very good dad himself.

Being a man is not about how many pairs of jeans you can steal. It's not about whether or not you can blow smoke rings. And it's not about making babies either. (Any dog, cat, or snake can do that.)

Prove greatness through what you are truly good at: creating art. Not machismo. Take advantage of what's already within you: raw, freaking, God-given talent. That's how to be a big man.

Don Tate

Don Tate has illustrated numerous critically acclaimed books for children including *Ron's Big Mission* (2009), *She Loved Baseball* (2010), and *Duke Ellington's Nutcracker Suite* (2011). Don is also the author of the book *It Jes' Happened: When Bill Traylor Started to Draw* (2012). His illustrations appear regularly in newspapers and magazines, and on products for children such as wallpaper, textiles, calendars, apparel, and paper products. He lives in Austin, Texas, with his wife and son.

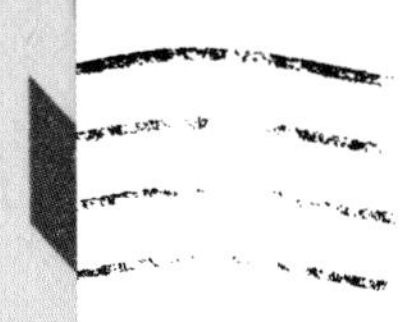

YOU'RE SO RIGHT BUT SO WRONG

Melissa Walker

Dear Teen Me,

You're right about almost everything. I know it and you know it. But the truth is, you're wrong about almost everything, too. Life is slippery that way, so let's break down some of your core beliefs:

You'll never get over your first love.

Why you're right: He's pretty awesome. He's hot, he makes you laugh, and he understands what you're thinking with just a glance. No one will ever know you in the same way that he does right now. There's no getting over a first love. There's only holding the memory of it close and making it a part of the fabric of the rest of your life.

Why you're wrong: Breaking up with him will not mean leaving yourself damaged in an irreparable way. You don't have to get over a first love, you just have to move on from him. And you don't have to rupture all your ties to him in order to do that. After the breakup, with a little time, you can even be friends again. (And by the way, I'm not just blowing smoke up your ass: You'll dance with him at your wedding, and he'll wind up being a close friend of your husband's.)

You'll never have friends this close again.

Why you're right: These people are hilarious and awesome and most of them have known you since you were five. It's hard to compete with that. The good news is, friendship is not a competition.

Why you're wrong: You'll make amazing friends in college and in your twenties, and you'll become even closer friends with them than you were with your high school friends, albeit in different ways. And they'll make you laugh just as hard as you did before. They'll all be additions, not replacements, so stop worrying about losing old friends.

You'll never be as popular as Lisa Shipley.*

Why you're right: In the context of the Chapel Hill High School hallways, she will always have more social cred.

Why you're wrong: I mean, who cares? She posts professional photos of her cats all over this thing called Facebook. I'd be willing to bet you that even in high school, when you envied her boyfriends and her loud laugh and her seemingly golden life, she felt the same way you do: inadequate, insecure, and worried that someone would find the chink in her armor. Hint: EVERYONE FEELS THIS WAY.

You'll move to New York City and become a writer.

This one, you're just plain right about. It took a lot of work to get there, but you're putting in the time because you love what you do. Nice job.

Now, in your thirties, you have a whole new set of things that you think you're absolutely right about. But you realize that you're probably wrong about a lot of them too. You've come to accept the idea that it's okay to be unsure of the future. It might even be better that way.

*Name changed, because we're Facebook friends

MCWalker

Melissa Walker is the author of six books including *Lovestruck Summer* (2009), *Small Town Sinners* (2011), *Unbreak My Heart* (2012), and the Violet on the Runway trilogy. She grew up in Chapel Hill, North Carolina (go Heels!), and now lives in Brooklyn with her husband and baby girl. She likes iced coffee that tastes like coffee ice cream and has saved every single mix tape from high school (for research purposes, of course). Visit MelissaCWalker.com to say hi.

DEAR TEEN ME

100% TRUE, GUARANTEED. BY TRACY WHITE

YOU ARE NOT STUPID, AND YOU DO NOT NEED "HELP" TO BE CREATIVE.

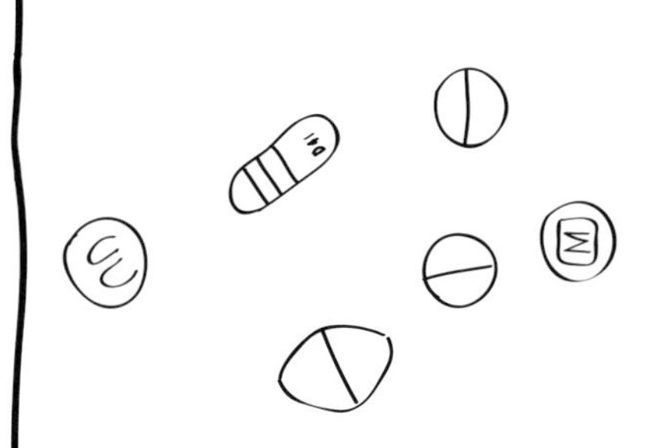

IN FACT, WITHOUT THE PHARMACUTICALS, YOU'LL ACTUALLY FINISH PROJECTS, LIKE THIS COMIC!

YOU WILL FIGURE OUT WHAT THE F. YOU ARE DOING HERE, AND WITH YOUR LIFE.

THE CLICHÉD SECRET IS TO LOVE YOURSELF. IT'LL BE YEARS BEFORE THAT HAPPENS, BUT IT DOES.

Tracy White grew up in and still lives in New York City. Her first graphic novel, *How I Made it to Eighteen: An Almost True Story* was a YALSA Great Graphic Novel, and an American Library Association recommended book for 2011. Her next book is mostly fictional, but this comic is 100 percent true. Find out more than you may want to know about Tracy at Traced.com. Yes, there are many more comics there.

ALL KINDS OF SEXY

Jo Whittemore

Dear Teen Me,

Right now you're dabbing on Charlie perfume and hiking your jeans *all* the way up—only inches away from camel-toe status. You're smart enough, *thank God*, to know that camel toe isn't sexy, but for some reason you think that supertight jeans are. Never mind that your pockets can't hold anything thicker than a stick of gum or that your legs hurt when you sit down.

You think you're sexy. And we can blame Janet Jackson for that.

She's all the rage at the moment, with "Rhythm Nation" and "Black Cat" topping the charts, and her music videos are hot. She's *sexy*, and you want to be sexy, too.

This means lace-up boots, tight clothes, and killer dance moves. Your specialty? The box step. You even diagrammed the moves, because nothing says "take me now" like drawings of feet and arrows. Unfortunately, you won't learn until years later that the box step is for ballroom dancing, but it explains why people at prom thought you were a complete dork. (There's now a reality show that makes ballroom dancing cool. You were simply ahead of your time.)

Looking back, I cringe at the other ways you'll try to be sexy: practicing a sultry lip bite (with buck teeth, you resemble a rabbit), hitting guys playfully on the shoulder (you hit harder than you think), and crossing your legs slowly à la *Basic Instinct* (you look like you have pelvic arthritis).

At one point, you'll even make sexy eating noises because you saw a woman do it in a yogurt commercial. The guy you're dating will laugh—*hard*—and ask why you're trying to be sexy with a rotisserie chicken. Even though he turns out to be a douchebag, he was right about the chicken. Don't eat poultry like that.

Then a strange thing will happen. You'll give up trying to be sexy, because the attitude that goes with it just isn't you. And you'll miss being able to carry stuff in your pockets.

This attitude shift makes me proud.

What doesn't make me proud is how far in the *opposite* direction you'll go, with hoodies and backward ball caps, like you're gangsta for life.

"Why bother at all?" you'll think. "Nobody will ever find me sexy."

And it's just not true.

Once your best friend convinces you to throw away the ball cap and brush your hair, you'll discover a happy medium. You'll grow more comfortable in your own skin and start showing your sense of humor. Clever one-liners will be your way to break the ice with strangers. Funny anecdotes about your past will turn these strangers into friends.

And guys will start to notice you more.

Because, apparently, humor is also sexy. A girl who can laugh at her own shortcomings and be herself is just as hot as one who can synchronize her arm and leg movements.

In fact, there are all kinds of sexy: smart, funny, sporty, tough...

And it fits all sizes, all shapes. Sexy is *you*, the real you. Why be anyone else?

Plus, in ten years, Janet Jackson shows her boob at the Super Bowl. Do you really want that much exposure?

Jo Whittemore

Jo Whittemore is the author of the humor novels *Front Page Face-Off* (2010), *Odd Girl In* (2011), and *D Is for Drama* (2012), as well as the Silverskin Legacy fantasy trilogy. She maintains a committed level of awkwardness that gets her invited to parties but never to the White House. When she isn't writing, Jo spends her time with family and friends in Austin, Texas, dreaming of the day she can afford a chocolate house with toffee furniture. And her own rhythm nation.

WHAT IS A FRIEND?

Sara Zarr

Dear Teen Me,

So you learned how to make friendship bracelets. Cool. They're very cute, and making them will keep your hands busy during those late-night babysitting gigs when the only other option is raiding the fridge. (Speaking of Things to Do While Babysitting, please stop watching movies like *Poltergeist* and *The Amityville Horror* when you're alone in a dark house! Just because this family has HBO doesn't mean you have to watch it.)

I just want you to think about this: What is a friend?

It can be hard to know sometimes. The nature of friendship changes as you move toward adulthood.

Childhood friendships were often based on proximity, what you like to do for fun, how your moms feel about each other. Don't get me wrong—a couple of those childhood friendships were great, memorable, so much fun, and so important. Rachel, for example. And of course Christine, who you'll still be in touch with when you're forty—and even though you aren't best, best friends like you were in childhood, it feels so good to still be known by someone who knew you when you were four.

As you get older, what you're really looking for is someone who understands you, with whom you feel a flash of recognition and a sense of home. And Sara? I'm going to tell you this, and it's not a criticism: You are not a person who is easily understood—by yourself or by others. But being understood matters enough to you that you'll go through a lot of pain and work to know yourself, and you'll make some missteps in your efforts to be known by others.

I'm not going to tell you about those missteps, though, or warn you against them. Each misstep shows you something about yourself that you needed to know, and refines your vision of what you want in a friend, which brings you closer to finding those people, that person.

As for what makes a friend, there's no ultimate definition. Friendships come in a lot of shapes and sizes. There are friends that are perfect for eating lunch with, friends you meet in a mutual endeavor—like at work or in theater or music—friends to party and play with, friends who are good companions on road trips. The longevity of these types of friendships tends to be limited by their context, but there's no shame or failure in that.

If there is any definition of a True Friend, maybe it's this: a person who understands the kind of person you want to be, and whose words and actions toward you are always guided by that understanding.

I do want to tell you what a friend isn't, though I know you're going to have to do the work of figuring this out on your own: A friend isn't a person whose attention and approval you depend on to feel okay about yourself.

This is a hard one to work out. Because Dad rejected you—not outright, not intentionally, but through neglect and the effects of alcoholism—some injured part of you is always going to be looking for someone (usually a man but not always) to make you feel okay. Even if everyone in the world tells you that *you're okay* (and you are going to have a great career that earns you a lot of attention and approval), sometimes it's not going to feel like enough.

This is going to lead to pain.

I sort of wish I could save you from that pain, but to paraphrase C. S. Lewis, the pain now is part of the joy later. And there's going to be joy, too, in the very midst of pain, because you are going to be blessed with a number of very meaningful friendships—some of which began from that place of needing approval but then grew beyond that and became real.

However, not all of them are lasting, and even though you'll think you're going to die when some of those friendships come to an end, you won't. You'll come out alive, stronger, better for the years that you had together, full of self-knowledge you wouldn't have discovered any other way. And self-knowledge is going to be really important for the work that you'll end up doing.

No, I can't save you from pain. But maybe you could at least think about these words from Naomi Shihab Nye when you're trying to discern who to share yourself with:

You Have to Be Careful.
You have to be careful telling things.
Some ears are tunnels.
Your words will go in and get lost in the dark.
Some ears are flat pans like the miners used
looking for gold.
What you say will be washed out with the stones.

I do have good news for you. Despite that injured part of you that sometimes gives too much of yourself away to the wrong people, despite being gun-shy because of past friendship debacles, when you're—no, you know what, I'm not going to tell you when or how or with whom this is going to happen. The utter unexpectedness of it all is part of what you will love, part of what will be so—I'm sorry, I know this sounds kind of woo-woo—so *healing*.

I'll just say: It's going to be sweet. There may even be friendship bracelets involved. And here's the rest of that poem, my promise from me to you. Me.

You look a long time till you find the right ears.
Till then, there are birds and lamps to be spoken to,
a patient cloth rubbing shine in circles,
and the slow, gradually growing possibility
that when you find such ears,
they already know.

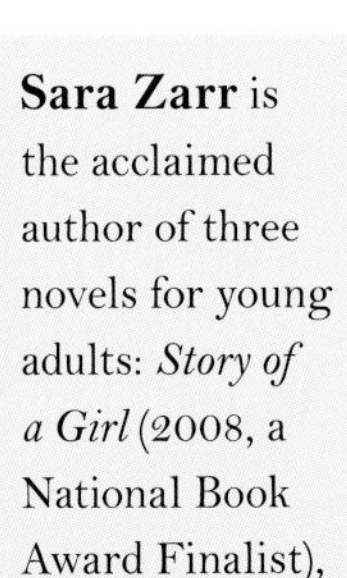

Sara Zarr is the acclaimed author of three novels for young adults: *Story of a Girl* (2008, a National Book Award Finalist), *Sweethearts* (2009, a Cybil Award Finalist), and *Once Was Lost* (2009, a Kirkus Best Book, Utah Book Award winner, and INSPY winner). Her short fiction and essays have appeared in *Image, Hunger Mountain online, Response,* and several anthologies. Sara's fourth young adult novel, *How to Save a Life*, was published in fall 2011. She lives in Salt Lake City with her husband. You can find her online at SaraZarr.com.

FACING FACTS: MAKEOVERS DON'T CHANGE A THING

Jennifer Ziegler

Dear Teen Me,

Back away from the curling iron! Back away now!

I know, I know. You're going for the über-tousled Belinda Carlisle look. Wild random curls that will reveal a confidence you don't yet possess and a madcap personality you'll never have. Why do you bother? You know very well that by your 10:00 am history class, your hair will be as limp as a mop's head.

Your tenacity is to be admired, however. You're like a physicist, experimenting day after day, trying to hit upon that magical combination of heat and hair spray that will allow your dishwater-blond locks to defy gravity—and genetics. But believe me, nothing will work.

You have straight hair, sweetie. Not sleek, shiny Pocahontas straight either. Straight meaning that it just hangs there, curl-free, but with enough kink to thwart the Indian princess look. At least you're not alone in your failings. Your school is full of fine-haired girls drooping out of their Madonna headbands.

What? What's that you're saying? A home perm?!

Dear God, no! Their toxic contents will mutate you into a longwool sheep! On especially humid days, your hair will have lift without curl. You'll be a walking Chia Pet! Put it down! Put it down, I say!

Now let's talk makeup.

Again, you're going for the look of an MTV pop star—but the end result is more...scary clown. Boy George instead of Pat Benatar.

Since you started kindergarten at age four, you've been a year younger than your classmates, and you were baby-faced to begin with. But smearing your lids with four different eye shadow shades and wearing dark lipstick doesn't make you seem older—it makes you look like a Madam Alexander doll someone marked up with crayons.

Here's the deal: You mistakenly believe that perfect looks will translate into a perfect, problem-free life. Only there's no such thing as a perfect face. And everyone has difficulties—always. But guess what? You can still be happy.

Poise doesn't come out of a bottle. True confidence comes from succeeding as yourself—wilted hair and all. Soon you'll recognize that your real friends love you no matter what the day's frizz factor may be. And those guys you like? They *really* don't care about your hairstyle. (Well, there is that one guy in drama class who loves to discuss beauty products with you. He's cute, yes, but trust me—he's not for you.)

So instead of trying to copy celebrities, just...be you. Put away the styling tools and twenty-five-color eye shadow kit. Make peace with your hair and let your real face show (or at least go light and neutral with the makeup).

Here are some bonuses to taking my advice:

You won't have to get up at 6:00 am to battle your hair and do your twelve-step cosmetic routine.

You'll save money.

The boys will appreciate not getting Revlon "Cherries in the Snow" on their lips when they kiss you. (And they will kiss you.)

Remember, I believe in you. In a sense, then, you already do, too. So act like it!

J Ziegler

© Erica Eynouf

Jennifer Ziegler is still no good at wearing makeup, still has bad hair days, and still has burn marks on her hand from high school curling wands. In college her hairstylist talked her into a "subtle red rinse" and she resembled an Irish setter for months. She even tried the all-black-wearing, raccoon-eyed look—only to find that she's too giggly to be goth. She now channels her disillusionment into YA novels about identity and acceptance, including the titles *How Not to Be Popular* (2008) and *Sass & Serendipity* (2011). Please visit her at JenniferZiegler.net.

Acknowledgments

I've been writing the acknowledgements page for my first book in my head for so long now that I'm terrified of leaving someone out in the real thing. Dear Teen Me is a project that begins and ends as a community project. We couldn't have done this on our own.

First I want to thank Miranda Kenneally, without whom this whole thing would have been just a pile of disorganized emails and a neon Tumblr. Seriously. This lady is so talented and I'm so privileged to work with her.

And then I want to thank every single author who said "yes" when I sent that first email. Without your willingness to share your stories on the Real Live Internets, we would have had a very bright but also very empty Tumblr feed.

Of course, I have to also thank the authors I was with at Spider House café in Austin when I sent out that initial email: P.J. Hoover, Jessica Lee Anderson, and K.A. Holt. Thank you so much for encouraging me (and convincing me that Dear Teen Me wasn't a crazy idea in the first place). You've got my back! Thanks also to all of the other writers at #THEPLACE who have supported me throughout this project: Madeline Smoot, Stephanie Pellegrin, Mari Mancusi, Cory Putman Oakes, Jennifer Ziegler, and Bethany Hegedus. You're amazing.

Thanks to Hallie Warshaw, who found me in the exhibit hall at ALA and thought our blog sounded like it would be a great book. The rest of Team Zest, too! Not to mention Sara Megibow, who has guided us so thoughtfully throughout this process. Sara, you're a gem!

And where would I be without my home team? Nikhil, my heart, my number one support—thank you for staying up late with me, for bringing home junk food, for tolerating the paperback takeover of our home. Thank you for listening to me read aloud, for keeping the lights on, and for holding my hand. Misha and Tim, you're the best friends a girl could ask for. And Ali and Megan, too! Thank you all for being as excited about this book as I am, and for pretending to be interested even when I talk about the boring parts of publishing. Emma, Sarah, Amber, my online critique partners—your support means the world to me, no matter where in the world you are!

Last but not least, my family. I wouldn't be doing what I love today without the love and encouragement I was given as a child, as a teen, and as a young woman. I'm lucky to have had family who nourished my wild dream of becoming an author. Mom, Dad, Joe, Allie, Nini, Papa, and Grammy—I can't wait to share this book with you.

—E. Kristin Anderson

First, thank you to E. Kristin Anderson (Emily) for all her hard work on Dear Teen Me. The Dear Teen Me project was her vision and I am grateful for her creativity, energy, and great attitude.

Also, Dear Teen Me wouldn't exist without the incredible authors who have contributed to the blog and anthology—thank you for sharing your stories with teens everywhere. I am also most grateful to the fans who read the Dear Teen Me blog on a daily basis.

I owe a huge debt of gratitude to my agent, Sara Megibow, and everyone at Nelson Literary Agency, for everything they do for me. Sara—you rock! I also need to thank all the awesome people at Zest—Hallie Warshaw, Dan Harmon, Tanya Napier, and Pam McElroy—thank you so much for your excitement, encouragement, and dedication to the project. Thanks to Holly Longstreth and Zach Dresher for keeping us organized. Last but not least: The biggest thank you goes to my husband, Don, who not only supports me in everything I do, but helped us to manage the website along with all the files and photos for the book. It was a huge undertaking he did not need to take on, but he did, and I am most appreciative. I love you, Don.

—Miranda Kenneally